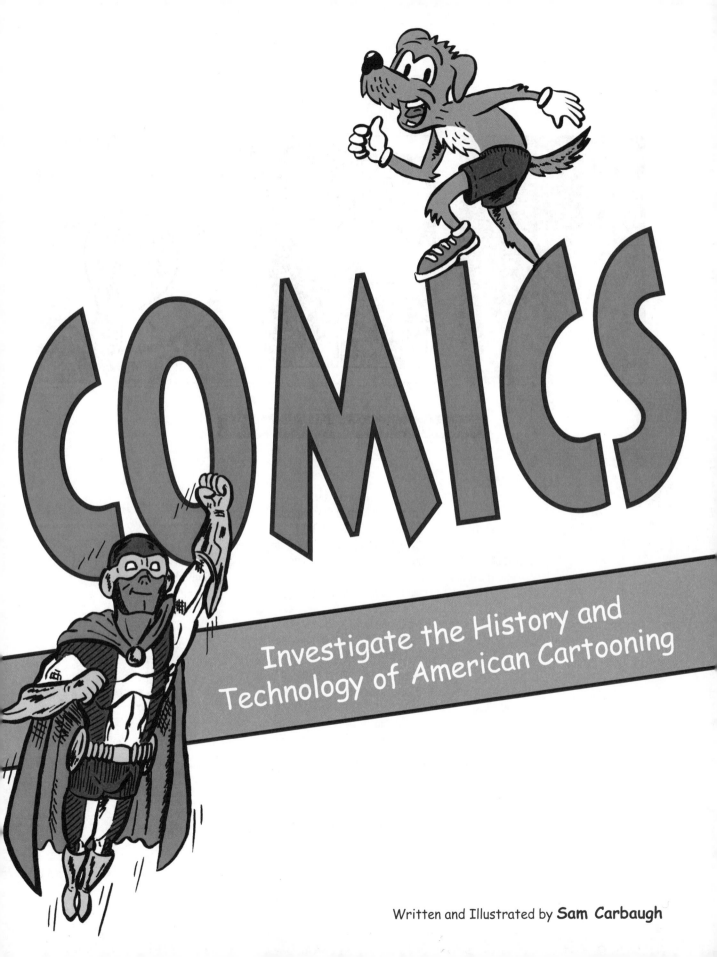

COMICS

Investigate the History and Technology of American Cartooning

Written and Illustrated by **Sam Carbaugh**

~ Latest titles in the *Build It Yourself* Series ~

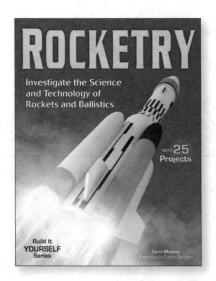

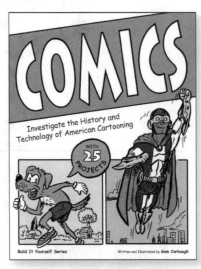

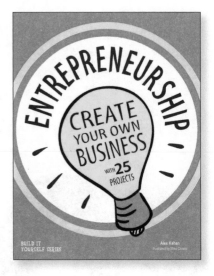

Check out more titles at www.nomadpress.net

Nomad Press
A division of Nomad Communications
10 9 8 7 6 5 4 3 2 1

This book was manufactured by TC Transcontinental Printing,
Beauceville, Québec, Canada
October 2014, Job #67327

ISBN Softcover: 978-1-61930-254-9
ISBN Hardcover: 978-1-61930-250-1

Illustrations by Sam Carbaugh
Educational Consultant, Marla Conn

Questions regarding the ordering of this book should be addressed to
Nomad Press
2456 Christian St.
White River Junction, VT 05001
www.nomadpress.net

Printed in Canada.

CONTENTS

PS **Interested in Primary Sources?**
Look for this icon.

You can use a smartphone or tablet app to scan the QR code and explore more about comics and cartooning! Cover up neighboring QR codes to make sure you're scanning the right one. If you don't have a QR code scanning device, you can find a list of each url in the Resources on page 118.

ABOUT 14,000 BCE

Ancient humans paint their stories and dreams on the walls of caves. The cave paintings in Font-de-Gaume, France, are among the most famous.

4000 BCE

Egyptians develop a pictographic language called hieroglyphics. They use hieroglyphics to tell stories about the gods and royalty.

200–900 CE

The Maya create the first codices, which tell stories about the lives of the Maya people, their religious rituals, and wars.

1000

The Cloth of St. Gereon is created. It is the second earliest known tapestry in Europe.

1430

Johannes Gutenberg invents the first movable type printing press in Europe.

1508–1512

Michelangelo paints the Sistine Chapel with help from "cartone" artists, the first "cartoonists."

1770

Paul Revere draws and then engraves the famous Boston Massacre illustration. This political illustration helps spark the American Revolution.

1812

Hokusai creates sketchbooks of manga drawings.

1840

William Sharp creates the first American chromolithograph. Future color printing processes are based on chromolithography.

TIMELINE

1875

Robert Barclay invents the color offset printer using CMYK color process to reproduce color images in large quantities.

1895

Joseph Pulitzer signs Richard F. Outcault to create the first serial comic for his newspapers, *The Yellow Kid*. When Pulitzer puts the first Sunday comics supplement into his newspapers, the funny pages are born.

1907

Bud Fisher creates the modern comic strip with *A. Mutt*. A few years later he introduces the first repeat comic sidekick, Jeff.

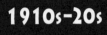

1910s–20s

Cartoonists such as George Herriman, Winsor McCay, Frank King, and others create some of the first and most experimental comic strips of all time.

1924

Harold Gray creates *Little Orphan Annie*.

1930s–50s

The Golden Age of comics, also known as the "Pre-Code" years. Comics created during this time are published for all audiences with no regulation.

1932

Jerry Siegel and Joe Shuster publish *Superman* in Action Comics. A year later, Bob Kane's *Batman* is published in Detective Comics.

1940

Timely Comics, the company that will become Marvel, publishes *Captain America*.

1949

The first Xerox photocopy machine is sold. It sparks a copying revolution, and is the most popular way to reproduce documents.

1950

Charles Schulz's comic strip, *Peanuts*, is first published. The strip's main character, Charlie Brown, and his dog, Snoopy, become two of the most popular comic strip characters of the twentieth century.

1954

The U.S. Senate holds hearings on the dangers of comics. Before the findings of the hearings are published, the major publishers of comics in America create the Comics Code Authority system to self-regulate their content.

ARE COMICS A BAD INFLUENCE ON THE YOUTH OF TODAY?

1956–1970s

The Silver Age, or "Code" years, of comics. It is marked by silly story lines and a cultural understanding that comics are only for little kids.

1960s

DC Comics and Marvel Comics create superhero teams. Marvel Comics become wildly popular for its unique, Atomic Age–style of hero. Underground comix are first published in several American college towns.

1963

American audiences see *Astro Boy*, their first taste of Japanese anime and manga.

1970

The Golden State Comic-Con is held for the first time. It will grow to become one of the best-known popular culture events internationally, the San Diego Comic-Con.

1970s

Comic books begin to break the Comics Code Authority, publishing comics for all readers, young and old. Zines and mini comics become popular. Independent comic book artists and writers publish their own work, taking advantage of the direct mail system to reach their readers.

1985

The first webcomic appears online.

1992

Art Spiegelman wins the Pulitzer Prize for his graphic novel, *Maus*. Image Comics is founded by former Marvel Comics cartoonists.

2000

Charles Schulz dies, having created 50 years of comic strips.

EARLY 2000s

Manga begins to outnumber graphic novels in bookstores.

2012

Marvel's movie *The Avengers* earns $623 million and DC's *The Dark Knight Rises* earns $448 million. They are the two highest-grossing movies of the year.

PEOPLE OF ALL AGES LOVE TO READ COMICS!

THEY READ THEM ON THE JOB –

– AND IN THE COMFORT OF HOME. COMICS, AND COMICS FANS, ARE EVERYWHERE!

SO, YOU WANT TO MAKE COMICS?

From newspapers to movie theaters, **comics** are everywhere. Your parents, grandparents, and even great-grandparents grew up reading them! They are one of the oldest ways to tell a story and they are one of the newest forms of modern art. Does that sound a little confusing?

Don't worry, in this book you'll learn all about the history of this fun art form and unravel some of the mysteries of comics.

What are comics? There are many definitions for comics floating around. The most universal one is that comics are **images** in **sequence** that tell a story, with or without words. A **cartoon** is a comic published in a newspaper or magazine.

WORDS TO KNOW

comic: images in sequence that tell a story, with or without words.

image: a picture of something, either real or imagined.

sequence: the order in which something happens.

cartoon: a comic published in a newspaper or magazine.

1

Words to Know

panel: a square or other shape that frames a single scene in a comic strip.

word balloon: a rounded outline with a point toward a character that encloses the character's speech.

thought cloud: a shape similar to a word balloon that encloses a character's thought.

narration block: a block of text that contains the voice of the writer or of a character talking about what is happening.

character: someone in a story.

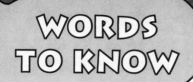

Like stories, comics have rules and systems to help readers understand what is happening. Instead of sentences, you can use **panels** to help contain an idea or scene. Pages of comics work like paragraphs, while **word balloons**, **thought clouds**, and **narration blocks** give your **characters** a place to speak, think, or observe.

COMICS DON'T READ LIKE STORIES OR NOVELS AND CAN BE CONFUSING IF YOU DO NOT KNOW THE RULES AND SYSTEMS.

Beginning

Narration Block

Panel

Middle

Word Balloon

Thought Cloud

End

Strip

Modern comics use panels to frame each section. These panels are arranged in a sequence, or order, from beginning to end. The first panel starts the story, giving basics such as who is in the strip and where the story is taking place. The middle panel or panels follows and moves the story along. The final panel ends the story and usually has something funny or exciting happen in it!

Comics are only as good as their characters. When you think of comics, do you imagine superheroes? The history of comics is full of different types of characters, from masked crusaders to funny animals. You can even turn yourself into a compelling comic character!

I LOVE COMICS HISTORY!

What makes a character interesting? Keep reading to learn how to make your own characters using some of the best techniques in comics!

Comics didn't just appear overnight with today's rules and systems. They developed into the comics we know now through years of experimentation. Advances in printing, duplication **technology**, and computers have also been important to the evolution of comics.

WORDS TO KNOW

technology: scientific or mechanical tools, methods, and systems used to solve a problem or do work.

Comics are fun and anyone can make them. As you read this book, you'll learn the basics of drawing, how to tell a story using comics, and how to make your very own comic book. You will even learn how to make a web comic that anyone in the world can read.

TRY THIS! Using stick figures, fill in the comic strip below. Make your characters speak, think, and observe in the right spaces.

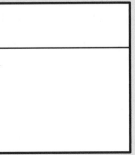

3

CHAPTER 1

PREHISTORIC MAN LOVED TO TELL STORIES!

THEY ALSO LOVED TO TELL THEIR STORIES USING PICTURES THEY PAINTED ON CAVE WALLS.

THE STORIES WERE ABOUT HUNTING, ANIMAL MOVEMENT, AND EVEN DREAMS.

ANCIENT COMICS

Where do comics come from? Ancient cave paintings in Font-de-Gaume, France, are some of the oldest paintings that we can still see. They are more than 14,000 years old. Sometime in the far past, the first human artists decided to tell stories of dreams and hunting by painting **representations** of things on the walls of the cave.

representation: showing things in pictures or other forms of art.

WORDS TO KNOW

The artists used simple lines to represent what they saw in the world and in their dreams. Humans on cave walls look a lot like the stick figures of today. Other animals are easy to recognize, such as reindeer and saber-toothed tigers.

WORDS TO KNOW

THESE PAINTINGS DON'T JUST SHOW PEOPLE AND ANIMALS STANDING STILL—THEY TELL A STORY.

tribe: a large group of people with common **ancestors** and **customs**.

ancestor: someone from your family who lived before you.

custom: a way of living and doing things, such as food and dress.

orally: spoken out loud.

generation: all the people born around the same time.

indigenous: native.

depict: to create a representation of something experienced or seen.

symbol: a physical representation of a thing or idea.

spiritual: religious, relating to the soul or spirit.

The humans are often shown hunting, throwing spears, and running. It's easy to imagine the artists sharing their stories with members of their **tribe**, pointing at these moments in the action to illustrate their story.

Until humans invented writing, most stories were passed along **orally**. The stories of the cave paintings of Font-de-Gaume were told to **generation** after generation, long after the original artists and storytellers had died. These paintings are some of the first examples of humans using images to tell a story!

MODERN DAY CAVE PAINTINGS

In Australia, many tribes of **indigenous** people use representational paintings to tell their stories. These stories often **depict** the dream countries claimed by each tribe. Using **symbols** for animals, rivers, trees, and rocks, the artists pass along the stories of their tribe to each generation. They also use their paintings when meeting with members of other tribes who have stories of their own. Most tribes use symbols from these dream paintings to distinguish themselves. By studying these dream country paintings, we can better understand how early humans used pictures to represent the **spiritual** dreams of their tribes as well as actual events in their lives.

5

WORDS TO KNOW

BCE: put after a date, BCE stands for Before Common Era and counts down to zero. CE stands for Common Era and counts up from zero. These non-religious terms correspond to BC and AD. This book was published in 2014 CE.

civilization: a **community** of people that is advanced in art, science, and government.

community: a group of people who live in the same area.

monument: a building, structure, or statue that is special because it honors an event or person, or because it is beautiful.

pictographic: a picture of a word or idea.

ANCIENT EGYPT

The Egyptian empire (3050–332 **BCE**) was one of the most powerful and advanced **civilizations** in the ancient world. It was famous for its **monuments**, such as the Sphinx and the Great Pyramids of Giza. We know more about the Egyptians than many other civilizations because they loved to tell stories about themselves. These stories included words and pictures!

The ancient Egyptians began to develop a **pictographic** language around 4000 BCE. A pictographic language is one that uses common images and sounds to help form words. Their letters look like the things they describe.

The term for this Egyptian form of written language is **hieroglyphics**. If you were to look at hieroglyphics you would see birds, eyes, snakes, and many other familiar images.

WHEN ANCIENT EGYPTIANS COMBINED THESE SYMBOLS THEY FORMED WORDS AND SENTENCES.

Egyptians loved to use hieroglyphics on the walls and pillars of their buildings. They told stories using images too. One reason we know so much about how Egyptians **mummified** their **pharaohs** is because of these ancient "comics."

Egyptians often told the stories of their pharaohs inside their **tombs**. These stories were read in sequence and had images to help the viewer understand what was happening. The **process** of mummification was usually depicted, showing how the body was prepared for the **afterlife**. Mummification began with cleaning the body and removing the organs and ended with wrapping the body and placing it in a **sarcophagus**.

WORDS TO KNOW

hieroglyphics: a writing system that uses pictures and symbols called hieroglyphs (or just glyphs) to represent words and ideas.

mummify: to **preserve** a dead body so it doesn't **decay**.

preserve: to keep something from rotting.

decay: to rot.

pharaoh: the title for ancient Egyptian kings or rulers.

tomb: a room or place where a dead person is buried.

process: an activity that takes several steps to complete.

afterlife: the ancient Egyptian belief in life after death.

sarcophagus: a large, stone box containing an Egyptian king's coffin and mummy.

7

MAYA: CREATORS OF THE FIRST COMIC BOOK

It may be a stretch to compare a Maya **codex** to a comic book, but the similarities are there. The Maya codices were created between 200 and 900 CE by the Maya people. Hundreds of years later, many experts are working to decode the Mayan written language. Thanks to the Maya codices and other **artifacts**, we are able to understand many things about their civilization.

The codices are brightly colored and use the inner bark of wild fig trees as paper. Some are the size of modern books with the pages folded together to be read. Other codices unfold into huge stories that could easily cover a wall. Each codex used words and pictures to tell stories about the Maya people.

One of the most common themes in the Maya codices is the stars. The Maya were famous for their ancient **astrologers**, who recorded the movements of the stars to help the Maya figure out the best time to do things. For example, the movement of the planet Venus was used by Maya astrologers to help their rulers decide when to go to war.

THE WORD "MAYAN" REFERS TO THE LANGUAGE OF THE MAYA PEOPLE. THE WORD "MAYA" IS USED TO DESCRIBE EVERYTHING ELSE.

8

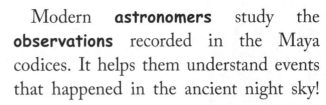

astronomer: a person who studies objects in the sky, such as stars and planets.

observation: something you notice.

scribe: a person who copies writings by hand.

archaeologist: a scientist who studies ancient people through the objects they left behind.

ritual: something done as part of a religion.

WORDS TO KNOW

Modern **astronomers** study the **observations** recorded in the Maya codices. It helps them understand events that happened in the ancient night sky!

The largest Maya codex is known as the Madrid Codex. It is one of the most complete codices we have from the Maya people. The book was probably written by more than eight **scribes**.

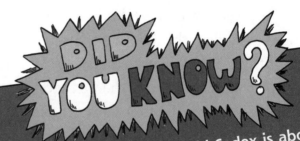

DID YOU KNOW?

When unfolded, the Madrid Codex is about 39 feet (12 meters) long. That's almost as long as a school bus! Since the book is drawn on both sides there are more than 78 feet (24 meters) of drawings and writing!

While the Mayan written language is still a mystery, the way the images are presented in sequence have helped modern **archaeologists** understand what they were trying to say. The Madrid Codex contains many astronomical observations, just like the other codices, but it also shows religious **rituals**, how to keep bees, and the art of Maya weaving.

tapestry: a colorful, woven fabric that hangs on a wall. It often shows a scene.

cathedral: a large important church.

TAPESTRIES: COVER YOUR WALLS IN STORIES

In Europe during the Middle Ages (350–1450 CE), lords and kings lived in huge drafty castles made of stone. To help keep the castles warm and to tell tales of brave royal family members, the walls were covered in brightly colored **tapestries**.

The second-earliest known European tapestry is 1,000 years old and is called the Cloth of St. Gereon. It shows bulls and griffins fighting, but no clear story. One of the earliest known tapestries to depict a story is from the **cathedral** of Halberstadt in Germany. It was made in 1175 and tells a story from the Bible.

TAPESTRIES BECAME MORE AND MORE DETAILED AS WEAVERS LEARNED NEW TECHNIQUES.

Many tapestries made for castles tell stories of the kings, lords, and knights who lived there. They tell stories without words and show scenes of war and daring. In many ways they look like modern superhero comics.

You can follow the story of St. George fighting a dragon or see King Charlemagne battle invading armies in Spain. Few tapestries have words on them, and even fewer show the lives of common people. Unlike the Maya codices, **medieval** tapestries focus only on the lives of the wealthiest people.

medieval: describes the Middle Ages, the period of European history after the fall of the Roman Empire, from about 350 to 1450 CE.

WORDS TO KNOW

One of the largest and most detailed tapestries is the Bayeux Tapestry. It is 230 feet long and 20 inches tall (70 meters by 51 centimeters). The tapestry tells the story of the Norman invasion of England in 1066 CE by William the Conqueror. Told from left to right, the story gives details about the battles and struggles that resulted in the fall of King Harold of England. Some scholars think he was the basis for King Arthur.

DID YOU KNOW?

The word *tapestry* comes from the classical Greek word *tapetos*, which means "heavy fabric."

The visual storytelling in tapestries helped inspire the artists behind the next evolution of comics. Enter the broadsheet!

WHERE DID "CARTOON" COME FROM?

During the **Renaissance** (1300s–1600s CE), many master painters created large paintings on ceilings and walls called frescoes. These paintings were so enormous that a single artist couldn't do all the work. The process of creating these masterpieces led to the invention of the terms *cartoon* and *cartoonist*.

Michelangelo began the process by sketching out a pencil or charcoal version of the complete painting. The sketched images had to be much smaller than they would be on the finished wall or ceiling. He would then hire other artists to help him paint the work on the wall. These hired artists drew larger versions of Michelangelo's sketch on big pieces of cardboard. These cardboard drawings, or carta, were used as models for the full-sized image on the wall.

Afterward, the cardboard drawings were thrown away or reused. The artists who did this work called their drawings "cartone," which would come to be known as cartoons today.

Renaissance: a period of time in Europe after the Middle Ages, from the 1300s to the 1600s.

WORDS TO KNOW

MICHELANGELO WORKS ON A NEW MASTERPIECE.

HE INSTRUCTS THE CARTOONIST.

WATCH THE FEET NOW!

THE TRANSFER IS DONE CAREFULLY...

I DO SUCH SPLENDID WORK!

GET YOUR BROADSHEET

Humans have always loved stories with pictures. Until the invention of the European movable type **printing press** in 1430 by Johannes Gutenberg, books were all written and copied by hand. The only places that had books were castles and cathedrals. Most people couldn't even read!

But people loved to sketch funny scenes on scraps of paper or on walls. Someone with a funny drawing to share had to pass around the original or have someone copy the drawing by hand. This made telling stories through writing or drawing really time consuming.

Then came the printing press. The first book to be printed on Gutenberg's new press was the Bible. Gutenberg began to print picture stories too, known as broadsides. Broadsides got their name from being printed on one side of a large sheet of paper. They were then either folded and passed around or plastered like a poster on a door or in a town square for everyone to see. Broadsides were fairly cheap to make and very popular.

printing press: a machine that presses inked type onto paper.

WORDS TO KNOW

MOSES AND THE EXODUS

SINCE MOST PEOPLE DIDN'T KNOW HOW TO READ, MOST BROADSIDES WERE PRINTED LIKE COMICS.

Broadsides often told stories from the Bible or showed the **martyrdom** of a **saint**. They used the visual storytelling found in the tapestries of the rich, but told stories anyone could enjoy.

Broadsides eventually became broadsheets, the early form of what we know as newspapers. As more and more people became **literate**, the pages of broadsheets were filled with words. Eventually, the picture stories were pushed into smaller and smaller spaces on the page.

THROUGH BROADSHEETS, THE MODERN political cartoon WAS BORN.

THE COMICS ARE COMING!

Broadsheets were popular throughout Europe and the American colonies. Printers had power because they could make **pamphlets** and broadsheets containing new and different ideas. One of the most famous illustrations printed in a broadsheet before the **American Revolution** was one of the **Boston Massacre**, drawn by Paul Revere. The drawing shows British troops opening fire on unarmed Boston colonists. **If you were a colonist, how would this picture make you feel?**

The cartoon doesn't tell the whole story of what happened, but Revere's image was burned into the minds of American colonists. The American Revolution may not have happened if it wasn't for these brave printers and the work of their presses.

PAMPHLETS AND BROADSHEETS OFTEN EMPLOYED ARTISTS TO CREATE DRAWINGS THAT INFLUENCED THEIR READERS TO ACTION.

Paul Revere continued to make political cartoons and sketches during the American Revolution. He wasn't the only American cartoonist to create political drawings during this time, but his were among the most popular.

Political comics are usually shown in a single panel and use exaggeration and symbols to tell their stories. Often they are meant to influence their readers' thoughts about a political party or country. Paul Revere found that if he showed the British as the bad guys in his comics, he could get more Americans on the side of the **revolutionaries**.

DID YOU KNOW?

After the Boston Massacre, the eight British soldiers who fired on the colonists were taken to trial and defended by John Adams. Six soldiers were found not guilty. Two were given a reduced sentence of public branding. John Adams later became the second president of the Untied States.

American newspapers continued to print political cartoons after the revolution. Instead of the British, the bad guys in the comics were whomever the artist disagreed with. This could even include the president.

revolutionary: someone committed to fighting a ruler or political system.

WORDS TO KNOW

PAUL REVERE: PATRIOT CARTOONIST

Paul Revere was made famous by the Henry Wadsworth Longfellow poem, "Paul Revere's Ride." We all know the famous ride Paul Revere took through the Massachusetts countryside to warn everyone by calling, "The British are coming! The British are coming!" What many of us don't know is that Paul Revere was also one of America's first cartoonists.

content: the written material and illustrations in a story, article, book, or website.

WORDS TO KNOW

ONE IF BY LAND...

TWO IF BY SEA...

HOW MANY IF BY AIR?

A famous silversmith in Boston, Paul Revere often doodled funny drawings on scraps of paper in his spare time. He was known as a supporter of independence who met with other revolutionaries to plot how they could get the British out of the colonies. His skills as a doodler were needed when revolutionary broadsheet printers wanted to include more visual **content** for their readers.

Besides the Boston Massacre, Paul Revere drew comics during the American Revolution that depicted the British soldiers, the colonists loyal to the king, and the king himself as bad guys. The single panel form was Paul Revere's favorite way of making his drawings. He was one of the first American cartoonists to use a form of the word balloon. Characters were shown to "talk" with ribbons of words coming out of their mouths.

JAPANESE MANGA

In 1812, a Japanese artist named Hokusai began creating sketchbooks he called **manga**. These quick drawings often told stories of traditional Japanese life, from local fishermen to powerful military leaders called shoguns. Hokusai drew very quickly and captured the movement and expression of people going about their everyday lives. He saw his sketchbooks as a good way to develop skills for his full-time job creating stories on tapestries, scrolls, and silk divider screens.

manga: a term for Japanese-style comics.
culture: the beliefs and way of life of a group of people.

WORDS TO KNOW

Artists employed by his studio were required to make their own manga using Hokusai's techniques. Hokusai's drawings were kept and passed on to other Japanese artists, influencing the development of Japanese comics.

Today, Japan has one of the most lively comics **cultures**. Comics are made about everything, from funny stories to serious lessons about doing business.

HOKUSAI'S NAME FOR HIS DRAWINGS ARE WHAT THE PEOPLE OF JAPAN CALL COMICS TODAY—MANGA.

SIDEWALK CAVE PAINTING

SUPPLIES: *long dry sidewalk, colored chalk*

Ancient humans used simple drawings on cave walls to tell stories about hunting, dreams, and daily activities. You can draw stories just like the ancient cave people!

1 Think of a story from your life you would like to tell a friend. Did your family go on a special vacation or a fun adventure?

2 Break your story down into sections. It should have at least three sections: a beginning, middle, and end. Your story might have more. A story about learning to ride a bike might have five sections. Can you think what they would be?

3 Find a length of sidewalk with as many spaces as you have sections. If your story has five sections, you will need five sidewalk spaces.

4 Starting with the first sidewalk space on the left, use the chalk and begin to draw your story. You can use stick figures and simple drawings to show what is happening. Continue drawing your story on the other spaces of sidewalk.

YOU ARE A DAREDEVIL!

TRY THIS! How could you tell stories like this using different materials? What if you were on a beach or in the snow? What's the longest story you could tell? Try getting some friends to tell a story together. Have each person add a different detail to each section and take turns telling the story to each other.

MANGA-STYLE SKETCHBOOK

PROJECT!

SUPPLIES: *several sheets of 6-by-12-inch (15-by-30-centimeter) white paper, stapler, glue, 2 squares cut from cereal boxes each 6 by 6 inches (15 by 15 centimeters), 1 sheet of 8-by-14-inch (20-by-36-centimeter) colored paper, markers*

Hokusai made sketchbooks and filled them with drawings of what he saw each day. You can make your own manga-style sketchbook.

1 Stack the white paper. Fold the stack in half to make a square, unfold, and put three staples along the fold.

2 Glue the cardboard squares to each side of the colored paper. Leave ¼ inch (½ centimeter) of space between them. Fold the excess paper around the cardboard and glue it down.

3 Glue the first and last pages of your stapled pages to the left- and right-hand cardboard squares so that the glued edges are covered.

4 Decorate the cover. Add a title and the date you start. You can make more sketchbooks as you fill them up, numbering each as you go. Include a start and finish date on each cover.

TRY THIS! Can you make sketchbooks in different shapes? Try using different colors of paper for the cover and different types of cardboard to make your cover more durable! How would you make a pocket-sized sketchbook?

DRAW LIKE AN EGYPTIAN!

SUPPLIES: *paper, pencils, blue painter tape, large pieces of cardboard, scissors, paint, paintbrushes*

The ancient Egyptians loved to tell stories about everything their civilization did! They used the walls of their pyramids, palaces, and temples to tell their tales. Popular themes were palace life, beliefs, and even farming! Follow in their footsteps and use words and drawings to tell future generations about something you do everyday!

1 Think about something you do every day that takes several steps to complete, such as getting ready for school. On a piece of paper, draw out the steps, starting on the left side. If you need more space, tape on another piece of paper until you have finished with your steps.

2 Cut up the cardboard boxes into large pieces of cardboard. Find an empty wall where you can tape up your pieces of cardboard. Make sure there is room to fit everything you drew on the paper. If you needed to use more than one piece of paper in step one, make sure you use at least that many pieces of cardboard on the wall.

3 Just like the early cartoonists of the Renaissance, draw big versions of your steps on the cardboard. Use words above your images to tell your audience what is happening in that step. For example, if you drew yourself putting on your shoes you might write, "put on shoes, tighten Velcro straps."

4 After you have drawn large versions of all of your steps, go through and add color with your paint. You now have a step-by-step record of something you do every day!

THE ROSETTA STONE

The **Rosetta Stone** was a carved tablet that translated hieroglyphics into other known ancient languages. Long before the Rosetta Stone was discovered, archaeologists were able to understand a lot about the Egyptian people because of their use of images in sequence. While they were still closer to ancient cave paintings than they were to the modern comic strip, these Egyptian stories were another step to what we now know as comics! But, as you've seen, the ancient Egyptians weren't the only ancient civilization to use images in sequence to tell important stories.

WORDS TO KNOW

Rosetta Stone: a stone tablet written in 196 BCE telling the same decree using hieroglyphics, Egyptian Demotic script, and ancient Greek. The stone was fully translated in 1822, leading specialists to understand hieroglyphics better in the nineteenth century.

← Hieroglyphics

↙ Egyptian Demonic Script

↙ Ancient Greek

CHAPTER 2

COMICS IN THE NEWSPAPERS

Have you read a newspaper today? Look in any newspaper and you might find dozens of comics printed in their very own section. Comics such as *Peanuts*, *Calvin and Hobbes*, *Garfield*, *Get Fuzzy*, and *Pearls Before Swine* have all become household names thanks to their presence in newspapers.

WORDS TO KNOW

innovation: a new creation or a unique solution to a problem.

smock: a cloth worn over clothing to protect it from stains.

Comics like these didn't exist in early American newspapers. Early comics were usually political cartoons such as those drawn by Paul Revere. It took the popularity and **innovation** of one political cartoon character to break open the gates for modern newspaper comics. This character was a bald boy in a yellow **smock**.

THE YELLOW KID

In 1895, Joseph Pulitzer was one of the most powerful newspaper publishers in America. He hired Richard F. Outcault to create the first **serial** comic strip character. Outcault's comic was called *The Yellow Kid*. The character wore a yellow smock with writing on it that stated what he was thinking or saying.

First **conceptualized** as a political cartoon, *The Yellow Kid* soon became very popular. Pulitzer published the comic on one entire sheet of newspaper using new printing techniques that allowed for cheap **color reproduction**.

The bright yellow of the kid's smock and the **humor** in the comic caught the attention of Pulitzer's readers. *The Yellow Kid* resembled old political comics and broadsheets since it rarely used panels, relying on one giant illustration to convey many jokes. For a while, *The Yellow Kid* was as popular as Mickey Mouse is today.

serial: occurring in a series.
conceptualized: imagined and thought out.
color reproduction: to make color prints of an original piece of art.
humor: the quality of being funny.

WORDS TO KNOW

I CAUZ A LOTTA TRUBBLE

THE POPULARITY OF *THE YELLOW KID* LED PULITZER TO FIND OTHER CARTOONISTS WHO WERE EAGER TO SEE THEIR CHARACTERS REACH A WIDER AUDIENCE.

PS

Richard Outcault's comics often took up an entire page of the newspaper and could be very busy and chaotic. **Take a look at this comic from 1896.** How is it different from the comics you find in the newspaper today? Is it easier to read? More fun to look at? Is it more confusing? Why do you think comics have evolved into their current, simpler form?

digital: characterized by electronic and computerized technology.
layering: stacking images on top of each other.
tint: a shade or variety of color.

WORDS TO KNOW

Pulitzer's main rival in the newspaper industry, William Randolph Hearst, wanted to include comics in his newspapers, too. He even tried to convince Richard Outcault to leave Pulitzer's newspapers and draw *The Yellow Kid* for Hearst's publications.

THE AMAZING COLOR PRINTER

Before **digital** printing was invented, most color printing was done using a process of **layering** the **tints** of four colors. This tricked the eyes of readers into seeing more than just the four colors. The process, called CMYK, is still used today. The colors are cyan (C), magenta (M), yellow (Y), and black (K).

EACH LAYER USES SHADES OF THOSE FOUR COLORS, WHICH, WHEN STACKED ON TOP OF EACH OTHER, CREATE WHAT LOOKS LIKE MANY DIFFERENT COLORS.

Early newspapers in America relied on **movable type** and **woodcut** images to print a single page. It was very time consuming! Large towns could afford to print daily newspapers, but small towns didn't usually have this luxury. Then, in 1843, an inventor named Richard March Hoe created the steam-powered drum printer, which took **castings** from a **master page**. It could print page after page from a large roll of paper. The drum printer made the printing process faster and easier.

In the 1880s, mass color printing was developed. This new color separation technique was called **chromolithography** and allowed newspapers to print comics and **etchings** of photographs in color for the first time. Newspapers flew off the stands!

WORDS TO KNOW

movable type: a process of printing that uses individual type pieces to spell out words.

woodcut: a way of printing by carving an image on a piece of wood before adding ink and printing the image onto paper.

casting: a metal print form created to make multiple copies of a printed page.

master page: the version of a printed page that is used to make other copies.

chromolithography: a color printing process using metal plates to layer tints of color.

etching: a print made by scratching original art onto a metal plate.

25

FACT OR FICTION?

Could the popularity of America's two major newspapers help to spark a war? A large part of the reason the United States went to war with Spain in the 1890s was because the public was influenced by articles written in Hearst's and Pulitzer's papers. The anti-Spanish articles were later found to be mostly false. The reporters had been actively encouraged to exaggerate their stories to help sell more newspapers! Do you think this could happen today? Why or why not?

THE FIRST SUNDAY COMICS

Joseph Pulitzer invented one of the most enduring forms of comics—the Sunday comics. First published in 1895, the Sunday comics were a collection of *The Yellow Kid* comics plus several others. The newspapers of the late nineteenth century were much larger than our papers today. The cartoonists often had an entire page to create their comics, and that meant a lot of creativity could go into each one.

Once Pulitzer proved that the Sunday comics increased sales, other publishers weren't far behind in publishing Sunday comics of their own. Newspapers started calling these new drawings the **funnies**.

Through the years, the Sunday comics have decreased in size, but they still remain one of the major selling points of newspapers.

WHAT'S YOUR FAVORITE FUNNY TO READ IN THE NEWSPAPER?

WORDS TO KNOW

funnies: the original name of comic strips in Sunday newspapers.

26

EARLY COMIC MASTERS

When comics first started appearing every week, newspapers were eager for new talent. Here are a few of the early masters of the modern comic **medium**.

Henry Conway Fisher and *Mutt and Jeff*: In 1907, Henry Conway Fisher, also known as Bud, introduced one of the greatest innovations in cartooning: the comic strip. Until then, most comics were huge splashes of color and action with few panel borders, such as in *The Yellow Kid*. Fisher decided to tell stories with **standardized** panels that were always the same size. Panels helped readers understand what was happening. The comic strip was also much smaller, which meant newspapers didn't have to use most of a page for just one comic.

Bud Fisher's comic strip, *A. Mutt*, featured a man called Mutt who got into lots of trouble. Hearst loved the work Fisher was doing and hired him to produce the strip for his national newspapers.

Look at the *Mutt and Jeff* comic strip that was reprinted in 1948. Is this the kind of humor people today would find funny? Why or why not?

sidekick: a character who supports the main character.
cast: a group of characters.
premise: the main idea of a story.
race: a group of people with the same skin color and other physical features.

WORDS TO KNOW

More *Krazy Kat*! PS

Along with inventing the panel, Fisher also introduced another innovation to comics: the **sidekick**. Bud decided to draw another character into his strip, a man called Jeff. The friendship between Mutt and Jeff was so popular that Fisher began to include him as a regular part of the story. He even renamed the strip *Mutt and Jeff.*

George Herriman and *Krazy Kat*: The first widely published African American cartoonist was George Herriman from Louisiana. Herriman's comic strip, called *The Dingbat Family*, began to appear in newspapers in 1910. The strip followed a **cast** of characters in an apartment building.

Krazy the cat and Ignatz the mouse were the most popular characters in the strip. One day, the mouse flung a brick at the cat's head. The cat took the brick as a sign of love from the mouse. This ridiculous **premise** appealed to readers, and Krazy and Ignatz eventually took over the daily strip. Herriman renamed the strip *Krazy Kat* and introduced a third character, a dog called Offissa Pupp.

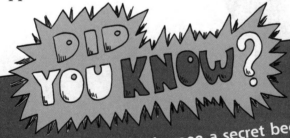

DID YOU KNOW?

George Herriman kept his <u>race</u> a secret because if people knew he was African American they might not read his comics. Do you think he would hide his race if he was drawing comics today?

Herriman played with the **logic** of the panels. Characters might find themselves in different seasons over the span of a few panels or they might chase each other around the moon. Eventually, inspired by the natural rock formations at Arizona's Monument State Park, Herriman modeled his imaginary world after the real Coconino County.

> **HERRIMAN WROTE dialogue WITH AN INVENTED SPELLING OF ENGLISH WORDS THAT REFLECTED THE SOUNDS OF SPANISH, YIDDISH, AND CREOLE ACCENTS.**

Krazy Kat was never a huge favorite with the general public. Many newspaper editors wanted to cancel the **eccentric** comic, but they couldn't since their boss, Mr. Hearst, loved it. It was also loved by many great artists and writers of the early 1900s, including the painter Picasso and the poet e.e. cummings.

OH MAH DAHLINK!
OH MAH DAHLINK!

THIS BRICK'LL HELP STOP THAT NOISE.

WORDS TO KNOW

logic: the principle, based on math, that things should work together in an orderly way.

dialogue: a conversation between two people.

eccentric: odd, usually in a unique way.

29

PS

Winsor McKay's comics were known as much for the artwork as the dialogue. Look at one of his comics from 1905. Where would a comic like this most likely be published today? In newspapers, magazines, or on websites?

rarebit: a type of soft cheese which is famous for giving indigestion.

WORDS TO KNOW

Winsor McCay and *Dream of the Rarebit Fiend* and *Little Nemo in Slumberland*: Winsor McCay began his career as a cartoonist drawing political cartoons, but he started making comic strips for his local paper after he saw how popular they were. His comic, *Dream of the Rarebit Fiend*, was an immediate success.

The exciting stories grew stranger and stranger until the final panel where the main character woke up. He blamed the strange dream on a cheese dish called **rarebit**, which he'd eaten before bed.

In 1905, McCay created *Little Nemo in Slumberland*. The strip followed the dream adventures of a boy named Nemo who was joined by a repeat cast of characters. With gigantic, colorful panels filled with inventive worlds, it almost always ended with Nemo waking in his bed and his father telling him to settle down. In one famous Sunday strip, Little Nemo dreams that his bed comes to life, the legs grow incredibly long, and it walks above New York City.

Little Nemo was wildly popular, and the inventive spirit McCay brought to his comic continues to inspire cartoonists today. While he was influenced by some of the art of his time, he was mostly inspired by the writings of **psychologists**.

Harold Gray and *Little Orphan Annie*: Harold Gray created the very popular *Little Orphan Annie* in 1924. The comic featured the adventures of an orphan girl with curly hair, a red dress, and large, blank eyes. Annie's eyes allowed readers to add their own expressions to the character.

Little Orphan Annie became an **iconic** image of the times. Annie was the foster child of a rich man, Daddy Warbucks, and they were always getting separated and having to find each other again.

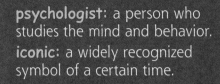

psychologist: a person who studies the mind and behavior.
iconic: a widely recognized symbol of a certain time.

WORDS TO KNOW

SIR, WHY ARE YOU STANDING UPSIDE DOWN?

DID YOU KNOW?

Annie's dog, Sandy, accompanied her on her adventures. Sandy helped popularize the idea of a non-human sidekick, something that would inspire other cartoonists, such as the creators of *The Adventures of Tin Tin* and *Calvin and Hobbes*.

COMICS

Little Orphan Annie was so popular that, during a newspaper strike in the 1940s, New York City Mayor Fiorello LaGuardia read the comic out loud on the radio so readers could keep up with her adventures. **Listen to the mayor's radio address.** Do you think the comic was as much fun to listen to as it was to read? How does the mayor include a lesson after reading the comic out loud to the audience?

Does *Little Orphan Annie* sound familiar? The popular comic strip inspired a famous musical called *Annie*, which has been turned into a movie and has been performed by thousands of schools and local theater groups throughout the country. Next time you find yourself singing along to "It's a Hard Knock Life," think about how it all started with a comic strip from the 1920s!

E.C. Segar and *Popeye*: Comics of the early twentieth century were packed with physical action. E.C. Segar's *Popeye* certainly had its share of fighting. Segar introduced Popeye as a side character in his popular strip, *Thimble Theater.*

WELL... SHIVER ME TIMBERS! I'MA MEETIN' ME MAKER!

THE 50-YEAR-OLD, ONE-EYED SAILOR WHO LOVED TO FIGHT EVENTUALLY STOLE THE STRIP!

Segar was surprised to discover the popularity of a character he hadn't planned on using for more than a few strips. Popeye's fame grew, and just as in *Krazy Kat*, the strip was renamed *Popeye* after the new main character.

Part of the popularity of *Popeye* had to do with the action sequences. The strip portrayed Popeye fighting a variety of **villains**, including his **arch-nemesis**, Bluto. Segar drew exaggerated scenes, showing the energy of each punch, kick, and wallop with the intensity of modern-day special effects.

villain: a character who opposes the hero and does bad things.

arch-nemesis: a character who is the opposite of the main character, and usually the enemy.

WORDS TO KNOW

MANY HISTORIANS THINK POPEYE WAS THE FIRST SUPERHERO. HE COULD PUNCH HARDER THAN ANY LIVING MAN, ESCAPE ANY TRAP, AND EVEN STOP BULLETS.

"I YAM WHAT I YAM"

Popeye ate spinach to get strong. His theme song even touted the strengthening powers of the green veggie, "I'm Popeye the Sailor Man, I'm strong to the finish because I eats me spinach, I'm Popeye the Sailor Man!"

The publishers of *Popeye* thought this was a great way to get kids to eat healthy. A decimal mistake made in 1870 made people think spinach contained much more iron than it really does. Spinach is healthy, but not as healthy as people thought before 1937, when the mistake was fixed!

THING, JOB, DESCRIPTION

Supplies: *pencils, paper, several friends, scissors, three cups, colored pencils or crayons*

Comics are about communicating ideas with pictures and words. A cartoon needs to convey important information to the reader without having to say it. For example, if your main character is a crime-fighting duck, your readers need to immediately recognize it as both a duck and a crime fighter.

As you do this exercise with a group of friends, keep in mind some key questions:

* ✱ What makes my animal look unique?
* ✱ What sorts of things give clues about my animal's job?
* ✱ How can someone tell what my character is feeling without words?

1 Make three columns on a piece of paper and label them "Animal," "Job," and "Description." In each column, write a list of examples. Write enough so each of your friends will get one from each column. For example, if you have eight friends, you would write out eight animals, eight jobs, and eight descriptions. These descriptions could be words such as clumsy, sleepy, or creative.

ANIMAL	JOB	DESCRIPTION
duck	police officer	brave

2 Cut out each animal, job, and description. Put the animals in one cup, the jobs in another, and the descriptions in the last one. You can fold up each piece of paper so that anyone picking out of the cup can't see what it is.

3 Pass each cup around the room. Everyone takes one piece of paper out of each cup. Once everyone has all three pieces of paper, get drawing with colored pencils and crayons! Make sure nobody can see what your combination is and remember, **don't use any words**.

4 Have each person show his or her drawing to the group and see how quickly people can guess what each of the drawings depicts.

OK, EVERYONE GRAB ONE JOB...

CAN YOU GUESS MY DRAWING?

TRY THIS! What helped people guess correctly? Did color play a role? Try adding a fourth category to the exercise. Also try replacing the categories with other things, such as vegetables instead of animals, or super powers instead of jobs.

DID YOU KNOW?

The struggle between Hearst and Pulitzer over who owned *The Yellow Kid* gave rise to the term yellow journalism. That phrase is still used today to describe the ridiculous issues that media outlets spend a lot of time on. Can you think of newspapers or websites that use yellow journalism?

DRAW CARTOON FACES

Supplies: *pencils, paper, good eraser, pen or thin marker*

One of the best ways to show emotion on a character is through facial expressions. The face may seem complicated to draw at first, but when you follow a few simple steps you can draw all kinds of faces! The best way to draw anything is by breaking it down into simple shapes.

1 FACE SHAPE: Most faces are oval, but some look angular. Draw a few different face shapes. Here are some examples.

2 GUIDELINES: Once you have a face shape you're happy with, lightly draw a vertical and horizontal guideline through the middle. These lines are very important. They guide us when placing the parts of the face.

3 NOSE: The nose is often used as a reference point on the face because it doesn't change shape as often as eyes, eyebrows, and the mouth. The bottom line of the nose is usually halfway between the horizontal guideline and the chin. Here are some sample nose shapes.

4 EYES: Every cartoonist has his or her own style of drawing eyes. But the darkest part of the eye, the pupil, almost always goes on the horizontal guideline. Here are some examples.

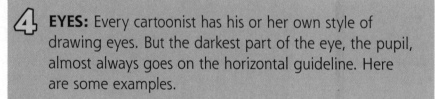

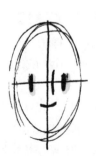

5 MOUTH: Lightly draw two lines straight down from the pupils of the eyes. At about halfway between the bottom of your nose and the bottom of the chin, draw your mouth. Start one end at an eye line and connect to the other.

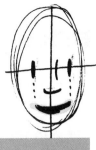

6 EYEBROWS: Eyebrows show the most emotion on a face. Look at the following examples and see how a blank face goes from normal, to mad, to sad, to tired, to surprised—all because of eyebrows.

7 EARS: To add ears, start at the horizontal line on the sides of your face. Curve up slightly before swooping around to the bottom of your ear. The base of the ear should be along the same line as the bottom of the nose. Take a look at the people around you. Do you notice how their eyes, noses, and ears all line up pretty much the same way?

8 HAIR: Start the hair a little below the top of the head. The biggest mistake people make when drawing hair is not connecting it to the head! Look at your own hair or your friends' hair. Which hairstyle will you choose?

9 Finish drawing the chin and trace over all the lines you want to keep with pen. This is called **inking**. Erase the pencil guidelines.

WORDS TO KNOW

inking: to use ink to add definition to pencil drawings.

DRAW CARTOON BODIES

Supplies: *pencils, paper, tracing paper, eraser, photographs of people that show the full body such as images from magazines*

Cartoon faces need to be attached to cartoon bodies to do stuff such as run, dance, sit, and fly. Get ready to draw cartoon bodies—bones first! Stick figures give us a general idea of where to put everything on our final drawing. Like the bones in your body, these lines give us a frame to build the meat of our characters.

1 Start with an action line. What's an action line? Think of it as the moving direction of your character. The middle section of the line will be your character's spine. Our character will be standing still, so our action line will be straight up and down.

2 Start at the top of your action line and draw your face shape, with the top of the line close to the top of the head. Don't make it too large since you need to add the rest of the body.

3 Just like faces, bodies can be drawn first as simple shapes. Let's draw a rectangle for the body. Then draw four circles, one at each corner of the rectangle.

4 Draw one line from each circle. These will be the arms and legs. Draw a circle at the end of each arm and a triangle at the bottom of the legs.

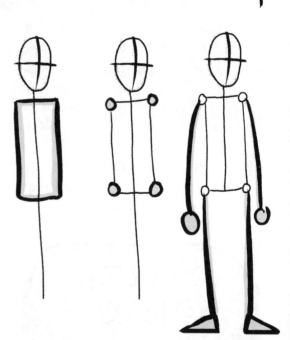

5 To make arms, draw two lines on either side of your arm line connecting the shoulder circle to the hand circle. If you want to get fancy, add an elbow circle and then connect shoulder to elbow and elbow to hand.

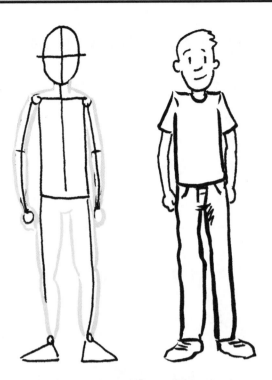

6 Repeat this process for the legs and neck. Erase the bone lines when you are done.

7 Clothes take a lot of practice to get right. Once you have the basic shapes of your body drawn out, however, you can hang clothing off of your character fairly easily. Add a simple T-shirt and pants.

TRY THIS! What body shapes do you see all around you? What is your body shape? Can you draw a full cartoon of yourself, face and body? Once you've mastered body shapes, try to draw different types of clothing on your characters. You can draw a bunch of dummy bodies and practice adding your fashions to them. Fashion designers do the same thing everyday!

TRY THIS, TOO! Now that you've mastered a cartoon body standing still, try to draw one in action. Look at people in different positions in magazines. Use tracing paper and try to find their action line, and then draw their sketchy skeleton. Try it on a bunch of different people and poses to see how your sketches change. Find some photos of kids and babies. Do their sketchy skeletons look the same as the adults? What's different?

DRAW HANDS AND FEET

Supplies: *pencils, paper, eraser, hands and feet*

Some parts of a character are really tricky to draw. The two that cartoonists struggle with the most are hands and feet. Here are some suggestions for tackling these tricky parts.

HANDS: Start with shapes. Most complex body parts can be broken down into a combination of basic shapes. For hands, think of circles and ovals.

1 To draw a hand with the palm up, first draw a circle. This will be the palm of the hand you are drawing.

2 Now, draw an oval on top of the circle where the base of the thumb goes.

3 Draw five finger lines. Make a shorter one from the thumb oval and four coming out the top of the circle— notice how they are different lengths.

4 Using simple guidelines, mark off the knuckle, just as you marked off the elbows and knees in the cartoon body project on the previous page. Then add some meat to the skeleton fingers. Erase your guidelines and marvel at your accomplishment!

FEET: Have you ever really looked hard at your foot? What shape is it? Artists tend to think of the foot as a triangle and a circle. You can also think of your foot as a wedge.

1 Looking at your own foot for reference, draw what you think the basic shape is, either a wedge shape or a triangle/circle.

2 Toes aren't as long or bendy as fingers, but they have distinct shapes. The big toe is a little farther away from the other four and is the base to your foot's arch. Start your toes by drawing little ovals for each toe.

3 Just as you did for the arms, legs, and fingers, add the outline to each of your foot's sketchy skeleton parts.

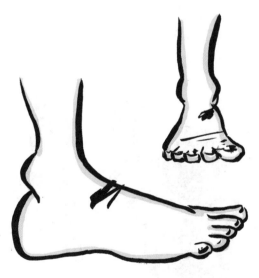

4 Erase your guidelines and enjoy! Next time, try drawing some shoes. How does this change how you think of a foot's shape?

TRY THIS! Whenever you find yourself with a little free time, you can practice drawing hands. You always have one with you! Like learning to play an instrument, drawing takes practice.

DESIGN A CAST OF CHARACTERS

Supplies: *pencils, paper, markers, small objects from around the house (such as vegetables, fruit, bottles, glasses, boots, and electronics)*

If you saw just a dark outline of your favorite cartoon character, you could probably tell who it was from its shape. Russell from the movie *Up* **looks like an egg, Popeye is skinny with a knobby head and huge forearms, and Sponge Bob is, well, a sponge! Interesting shapes make interesting characters. Practice making different characters out of everyday shapes.**

1 Arrange your objects in front of you and draw each shape on a piece of paper. Review all your shapes—look at them upside down and sideways. Do the shapes suggest any body types to you? For example, an upside down ketchup bottle may look like a football player with a big chest.

2 Once you have some body types in mind, start to figure out how to turn each shape into a character. Sketch out the face, where the pants go, and add arms and legs. Use what you've learned from the projects so far to bring your characters to life. Don't forget to give your characters names!

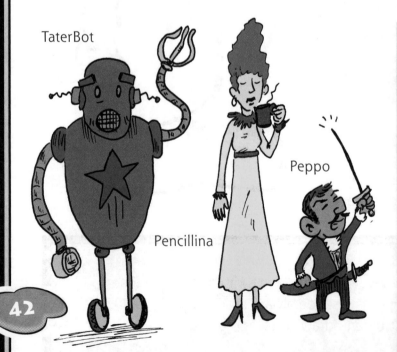

TaterBot

Pencillina

Peppo

TRY THIS! When you watch a cartoon or animated movie, have your homemade manga sketchbook handy. Pause the movie when a new major character is introduced. Try to sketch the shape of that character. Do different shapes tell you something about the character? What are heroes shaped like? What about villains?

SUNDAY COMIC STRIP

Supplies: *pencils, paper, ruler, pens, colored pencils, sketchbook with your character designs*

Now that you have an awesome cast of characters, it's time to show them off in a Sunday comic strip! Every good comic strip begins with a thumbnail. Not a real thumbnail! In cartooning, a thumbnail is a small sketch, or plan, of what your whole page will look like.

1 Start your thumbnail by making your comic strip panels. Draw a rectangle about 3 by 2 inches (8 by 5 centimeters) and then divide it up into panels. Use simple stick figures and rough word balloons to sketch out the action or joke of the strip. The beauty of thumbnails is you can erase them to change your ideas. You can even draw several thumbnails of each comic to try to find the best design.

2 On a fresh piece of paper, lay out your comic panels carefully with a ruler. Follow your thumbnail so that you have enough panels and they are in the right place.

3 Sketch out your characters and words with pencil first, then use your pen to trace the lines you want to keep. When you are done inking, erase the pencil.

4 Now you are ready for color! Be creative and don't be afraid to use lots of color. Give your masterpiece a title and sign your name!

TRY THIS! Design other Sunday comics using different shapes for the panels. Do circles or triangles make the comic funnier or more serious? Try making a comic with no words at all. Can you still tell a joke or story without words?

CHAPTER 3

THE BIRTH OF SUPERHEROES

Everyone loves heroes! Ever since ancient times, people have been telling stories about men and women with super strength who risk their own safety to save the lives of others.

epic: a long poem, usually about the life of a hero or heroine.

city-state: a city and its surrounding area, which rules itself like a country.

WORDS TO KNOW

The oldest hero to appear in an **epic** was Gilgamesh, a hero from a region of the world called the Fertile Crescent. This area is where the countries of Iraq, Syria, Kuwait, and Iran are today. Gilgamesh was very strong and helped save his **city-state** from monsters and villains.

One of Gilgamesh's first challengers was Enkidu, a powerful warrior whom Gilgamesh fought for weeks. Eventually, Enkidu was defeated and became Gilgamesh's friend. Enkidu was one of the first sidekicks!

Ancient Greeks also told tales about superheroes, such as Achilles, who had only one weak spot—his heel. Another hero, Odysseus, battled monsters on his journey home from war. Stories and poems from the past often featured very strong people who protected weaker people.

WHY WERE STORIES ABOUT SUPERHEROES POPULAR BACK THEN? WHY ARE THEY POPULAR NOW?

EARLY SUPERHEROES

Comic book superheroes have several **predecessors** other than the ancient Greek heroes. One of those is the Scarlet Pimpernel. Created by a Hungarian writer named Baroness Emma Orczy, the Scarlet Pimpernel was a **vigilante** who saved wealthy **aristocrats** from the horrors of the **French Revolution**. It is one of the first instances of a hero using a disguise and an **alter ego**, two common characteristics of modern-day superheroes, such as Batman. *The Scarlet Pimpernel* was made famous in America through a new form of entertainment, **pulp magazines**.

predecessor: someone or something that came before others.

vigilante: a person who takes the law into his or her own hands.

aristocrat: a person of royal blood or privilege.

French Revolution: a period of violent change in France between 1789 and 1799.

alter ego: a second personality in the same person.

invincible: someone who cannot be defeated.

pulp magazine: a cheap fiction magazine published between 1896 and the 1950s.

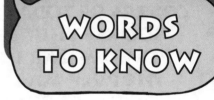
WORDS TO KNOW

DID YOU KNOW?

According to the story, Achilles's mother wanted her son to be invincible, so she dipped him in a magical river. But she held onto his heel so he wouldn't float away. That's where we get the term *Achilles's heel*, which means weak point.

45

science fiction: stories that deal with the influence of real or imagined science.

suspense: a feeling or state of nervousness or excitement caused by wondering what will happen.

WORDS TO KNOW

Pulp magazines were cheaply made publications that people bought for the exciting stories of romance, **science fiction**, adventure, westerns, and **suspense**. Many Americans were first introduced to characters such as Tarzan and Sherlock Holmes through pulp magazines. Other twentieth-century heroes had their start in the pulps, too, such as Buck Rogers and Zorro. The covers of pulp magazines were bright and flashy and would sometimes have nothing to do with the actual stories inside.

TAKE A LOOK AT THE COVERS OF TODAY'S COMIC BOOKS—THEY HAVE A VERY SIMILAR LOOK TO THE PULP MAGAZINES OF THE EARLY 1900s.

One of the most important science fiction pulp magazines was called *Amazing Stories*, which was about a future in which everyone had a jet pack or battled alien cultures on Mars. The cover of one *Amazing Stories* pulp shows a man flying through his neighborhood, aided only by a small device. It inspired a few important teenagers in Cleveland, Ohio, who created a superhero who would one day fly.

RADIO!

The early twentieth century saw the rise of a very popular new technology—radio! Radio programs, many of them inspired by pulp magazines, were **broadcast** across the country. From coast to coast, people could listen to the same shows. Some of the first radio **networks** are still around today, although they mostly do television. The Columbia Broadcasting System (CBS) and the National Broadcasting Company (NBC) are two of these. These radio broadcasts helped make three modern heroes household names: Tarzan, Zorro, and the Shadow.

THE FIRST COMIC BOOKS

The first comic books looked like the Sunday newspaper supplements. These collections of material that had already been published were simply stapled together with a flashy cover. Soon, actual comic book publishers began to create new content, such as comic **adaptations** of Bible stories or historical events.

Few people thought that comic books could ever be popular. Newspapers, movies, radio, and pulps—that's where people assumed they'd find excitement, action, humor, and **drama**. But they were wrong! A few key characters helped to make comic books very popular.

broadcast: a program transmitted over a long distance.

network: a company that provides programs to be broadcast over radio or television stations.

adaptation: telling a story in a different way and in a new format. For example, making a musical out of a series of comic strips would be adapting the comics into the musical.

drama: an exciting event or series of events.

WORDS TO KNOW

47

freelance: to work on a project without being employed by the company assigning the work.
brainstorm: to come up with a bunch of ideas quickly and without judgment.
pitch: to present an idea.

WORDS TO KNOW

One of those characters was Superman. In 1932, two buddies named Jerry Siegel and Joe Shuster were working as a **freelance** team. Jerry was the writer and Joe was the artist. Together, they **brainstormed** the idea of an alien who looked just like us, but had abilities above and beyond humans. They wanted their hero to be larger than life with an energy you could feel coming off the page.

Siegel and Shuster's idea was rejected by many publishers during a period of several years. Finally, they **pitched** their idea to a small publisher in New York City called Action Comics, which agreed to give them a try.

Superman first appeared as a man in a blue costume and a red cape with the letter "S" on his chest, lifting a car over his head. Superman wasn't the only story to appear in this iconic issue. However, he is the only character people remember!

Check out the very first Superman cover. The publisher worried that people would find the idea of a man lifting a car ridiculous.

The publishers of *Superman* found their second big seller the following year. A young cartoonist named Bob Kane was inspired by movies and pulp heroes such as the Scarlet Pimpernel. He pitched the idea of a wealthy man who, at night, dresses in a bat suit to rid his town of crime. In a 1933 issue of Detective Comics, Batman first swings into the world. He proved to be another popular figure and helped to introduce what would become known as the **Golden Age** of comics.

THE GOLDEN AGE OF COMICS

The superhero comic books of the early 1930s are the beginning of what many comics historians call the Golden Age of comics. It was golden because it was so new and popular. Everyone wanted to read comic books, both kids and adults.

Comics during this **era** expanded beyond their stapled pages and were adapted into movies, radio programs, and daily comic strips in national newspapers. Sales of comics made publishers rich and comics artists famous.

DID YOU KNOW?

In the beginning, things were a lot different for Superman. Sure, he was bulletproof, but he couldn't fly. Jerry Siegel reasoned that he could jump higher than the tallest building and have super strength because he was originally from a planet with stronger gravity than Earth! Also, Superman wasn't from the city of Metropolis—he was the protector of his creators' <u>hometown</u>, Cleveland, Ohio!

WORDS TO KNOW

hometown: the place where a person, thing, or idea is born.
Golden Age: the period of comics history before the 1950s, considered to be the best and most popular by many fans and historians.
era: a set segment of time.

THE BIG SCREEN

Like radio, movies took inspiration from pulp magazines. One of the first popular science fiction movie series was about Buck Rogers, a famous pulp fiction and comic strip hero. Most movies had live actors and actresses performing superhuman feats, but **animation** has always been popular, too. One of the most famous early animated films is an adaptation of E.C. Segar's *Popeye* by the Fleischer Brothers Studio. Never before had audiences seen the likes of Popeye, except in the funnies of course!

Watch one of the first animated movies of Popeye! How is it different from the cartoons kids watch today?

PS

animation: multiple drawings in sequence to show movement.
penciling: to create an original comic first in pencil.
dynamic: full of movement.

WORDS TO KNOW

There were no restrictions on comics in the Golden Age. They could be about anything and people still loved them. This level of comics popularity would not be seen again in America for nearly 50 years. A few comics artists stand out for being especially innovative.

Will Eisner: Will Eisner started his comics career **penciling** and inking for other cartoonists. Eisner decided to make his panels more **dynamic** by matching the shape and design of the panels to the action within them.

In 1940, Eisner was given the chance to create his own superhero. Unlike the other cartoonists of his day, he had complete control over how the story was told and how it was published. He retained all the **creative rights** to his creation. Called *The Spirit*, Eisner's comic followed the adventures of a former detective who was thought to be dead.

> **creative rights:** the right to use something that is created, often for profit.
>
> **Nazi:** the main political party of Germany before and during World War II.
>
> ## WORDS TO KNOW

Joe Simon and Jack Kirby: During the 1930s and 1940s, a new, small pulp publisher called Timely Comics needed a hit superhero to rival the popular Superman. Writer Joe Simon, who was also the head editor of Timely Comics, teamed up with an old friend of his, Jack Kirby. Together, they invented the next great American superhero—Captain America.

The first *Captain America* comic was modeled on the most talked-about news of 1940. Captain America was sent to do battle with the rising **Nazi** threat and Adolf Hitler himself. Would *Captain America* have been as popular if it had been published in a time of peace instead of a time of war? Why?

51

WORDS TO KNOW

splash page: large pages of comic action with no panels.

immigrant: a person who leaves his or her own country to live in another country.

inbetweener: an animator who assists the head animator by drawing movements in between key frames.

key frame: a drawing in animation that captures the major points of movement. For example, if a character is waving her arm from left to right, the key frames would show the arm on the left, middle, and right.

CAPTAIN AMERICA WAS AN IMMEDIATE SUCCESS.

The art and storytelling of Jack Kirby was unlike other comics of its day. Huge **splash pages** were used for the battle scenes. The characters were drawn as a cross between the flashy cover art of pulp magazines and the frenzy of newspaper comics such as *Popeye*. The comic world hadn't seen anything like it.

MORE ABOUT JACK

Jack Kirby was born Jacob Kurtzberg to Jewish **immigrant** parents. He grew up in a poor section of the lower east side of Manhattan and learned how to draw from copying the art he saw on the covers of pulp magazines. Eventually, he found work as an **inbetweener** for the Fleischer Brothers Animation Studio, filling in extra drawings needed between **key frames**.

After the animation studio closed and moved to Florida, Kirby became a freelance cartoonist taking on odd jobs to pay the bills. His two hit comics for Timely, *Captain America* and *Boy Commandos*, inspired many future comics artists to start their own careers.

DID YOU KNOW?

That small comic publisher, Timely Comics, would eventually grow up to be Marvel Comics, one of the best-known comic publishers in the world.

CARTOONING WOMEN

From the first decade of comics, women have been making comics for newspapers and comic books. In the 1920s, several women saw their comics published widely, and a few even got rich.

Edwina Dumm created a comic strip called *Cap Stubbs and Tippie* about the adventures of a young boy, his grandma, and Tippie the dog. *Cap Stubbs and Tippie* was one of the first comics made by a woman to be popular throughout America. It inspired a famous Halloween song and was eventually made into a weekly feature in *Time Magazine*, where the better printers allowed Dumm to create beautifully illustrated comics.

You may have heard of Kewpie dolls from your grandparents. The Kewpie doll came from a comic created in 1905 by Rose O'Neill. She told funny stories of little **cherubs** she called Kewpies. The comics were often colorful and were popular among adults and children.

Other women worked in comics and comic books throughout the Golden Age of comics, although many aren't widely remembered today. Their work, however, did inspire future generations of women who would make memorable comics of their own.

WORDS TO KNOW

cherub: a type of angel, usually shown as a small child.

HEROES GO TO WAR

World War II officially began for the United States after the surprise attack on **Pearl Harbor** by Japan on December 7, 1941. Thousands of Americans signed up to join the armed forces, including many of America's artists and cartoonists.

WORDS TO KNOW

Pearl Harbor: a U.S. naval base in Hawaii that was attacked by Japan in 1941.

Jack Kirby was sent to Europe, where his quick drawing skills were noticed by his commanders. They sent Kirby out as a scout to draw enemy encampments and artillery positions.

THE DANGEROUS JOB LATER INSPIRED SOME OF KIRBY'S MOST MEMORABLE COMICS.

WALT DISNEY AT WAR

Have you ever been to Disney World? Walt Disney also contributed to the war effort. His studios were commissioned by the U.S. Armed Forces to create short animated films for two purposes—to encourage Americans to buy war bonds and to educate soldiers about a variety of subjects. Walt Disney also led a team of artists that designed decals for the noses of American bombers and cargo planes.

Watch one of Disney's war **propaganda** films. How do you think people in 1943 responded to these movies?

PS

propaganda: ideas or statements that are sometimes exaggerated or even false. They are spread to help a cause, political leader, or government.

WORDS TO KNOW

Comic book characters also went to battle with America's enemies during this time. Batman and Superman helped to foil Nazi spies. Lesser-known superheroes such as Plastic Man, who could bend and fold into any shape, thwarted Japanese spy rings. Of course, Captain America continued his battles with the Nazi forces. The superheroes were widely read by American troops.

While comic book heroes and artists were going to war, they had an even bigger fight waiting for them when they returned.

THE GOLDEN AGE OF COMICS WAS COMING TO AN END.

DRAW A SUPERHERO

Supplies: *pencil, paper, colored pencils, digital camera, a friend (optional)*

Some of this may be familiar since we use basic shapes and action lines to make our superhero. But heroes are larger than life, and the same thing is true with drawing them!

1 Start with an action line. If you want your hero to be flying, draw a big swoosh instead of the straight action line you used for standing still. If your superhero is going to be bigger than your regular characters, make your action line longer. Draw the head shape at the top of the action line.

2 Skip a little down the action line to allow room for the neck, and then draw a large triangle for the upper body. If you are drawing a male hero, make it big. If it's a female hero, draw a slightly smaller triangle. Draw an oval where the hips will be, then add the socket circles for the shoulders and legs. Complete the skeleton arms and legs as you did in the last chapter.

3 Superheroes are also bulkier than regular characters. Add muscles to arms, shoulders, and legs. Go ahead and make them look exaggerated. Muscles make your character super!

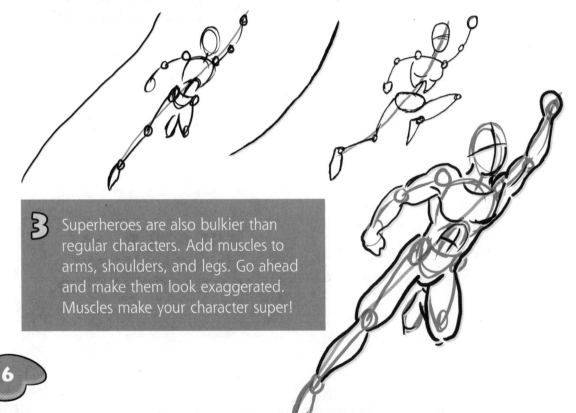

4 To draw the face, follow the same steps as before, but keep in mind that most superhero faces look more realistic than other comic characters. Look at your favorite superheroes' faces for ideas and try to make your superhero strong and expressive. Giving your superhero a mask or hood will make drawing his or her face easier.

5 Wait, what about clothes? Don't worry, you will outfit your superhero in the next project. But you can start brainstorming now!

TRY THIS! Most comic book artists use friends as models for their superheroes. Find a friend and use a digital camera to take some pictures of different poses. How could you take a picture of a flying pose without making your friend jump?

THE NAZI BAN ON COMICS

The Nazis thought that American comics were one of the most powerful propaganda tools the **Allied forces** had. Because of this, the Nazis banned almost all forms of comics and would not allow anyone to have anything that depicted American characters such as Superman or Mickey Mouse. The Nazi ban on American comics changed the direction of European comics in the twentieth century. Almost no European superhero comics exist today.

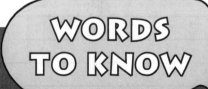

WORDS TO KNOW

Allied forces: the armies of the countries that fought together against Germany in World War I and World War II.

DESIGN A COSTUME AND BACKSTORY

Supplies: *pencil, paper, notebook, superhero drawings*

Think of Batman, Spiderman, Iron Man, The Hulk, Wolverine, and Wonder Woman. What do all these characters have in common? That's right, strong secret <u>identities</u> linked to their names and great costumes. Every great superhero needs a costume and <u>backstory</u>.

1. Brainstorm ideas for a name for your superhero. Make a chart with two columns like the one below. In the first column, list 10 nouns. These are people, places, or things. In the second column, list words such as man, boy, girl, or woman. Now try matching some of your nouns in column one with the words in column two. Do any sound cool or interesting? If you don't like any of the names you come up with at first, try another list of 10 until you find something you like.

NOUNS	
crash	
tower	boy
monster	
alien	girl
duck	
	man
	woman

2 Who is your superhero when he or she isn't busy saving the world? How did he or she get his or her powers? Conduct an interview to find out! Write a list of 10 different interview questions. **Here are some examples:**

* "What do you do for work?"

* "What do you like to eat for dinner?"

* "Do you have children?"

* "How old were you when you got your powers?"

3 Pretend to ask your superhero questions and write down what you think the answers would be. This will give you a more complete picture of who your superhero really is!

4 Superheroes need costumes! Make a chart with two columns. In the first column, list different situations your superhero might encounter, such as rescuing people at sea or stopping nuclear bombs. In the second column, name the costume piece or gadget your superhero will need, such as a cape, motorized swimming shoes, or an automatic heat shield. Choose which ones you want to give your character.

SITUATION	COSTUME NEEDED
escape tall building	cape
rescue people at sea	motorized swimming shoes
stop nuclear bomb	automatic heat shield

TRY THIS! Design a sidekick. How will the sidekick look compared to the main hero? Will the costume look different or the same? Why do you think some sidekick characters, such as Batman's Robin, look very different and more colorful?

DESIGN A VILLAIN

Supplies: *pencils, paper, markers with dark colors*

Every hero needs a villain! Originally, a villain was someone who lived outside of a village. Now, a villain is anyone who wants to upset the normal way things are done. Some villains want revenge. Others want to rule the world. As you design your own villain, think about your hero. Who would be the opposite of your hero? Why would your hero need to protect the world from the villain?

1 Come up with the shape of the villain. Villains are often the opposite of your hero. If you have a shorter hero, you may want the villain to be very tall. If your hero is really strong, the villain may need to look weak. Once you have a basic shape, draw the body as you would for a normal comic character.

2 Design the villain's face. Think of villains you have seen in animated movies. What sort of facial features do they have in common? One of the most expressive parts of a villain's face is the eyes. Look at some of the following examples to see how you can make a face villainous.

3 Just like your hero, villains need a good backstory. What made them villains? Do they have **diabolic** plans? Were they childhood friends with your hero? Were they once heroes themselves?

WORDS TO KNOW

diabolic: extremely evil.

4 Most villains have dark costumes. If you have seen any Disney films, you may have noticed that the villains usually have black and purple in their costumes. Play around with a few designs for your villain's costume.

TRY THIS! Villains usually don't work alone. They rely on minions or thugs to do their dirty work. Try to design a few minions or thugs for your villain. Design their costumes based on what you drew for the villain.

WILL EISNER

Will Eisner put comics to work for the armed forces. He was **drafted** into the service and began to draw for many army publications, most famously *PS Magazine*. He developed a popular character called Joe Dope who showed military men the wrong way to do something. It offered a humorous note to what was often boring content. The work he did during World War II inspired the Army to hire Eisner to create a comic book called *Preventative Maintenance* to be a part of *PS Magazine*. The comic showed soldiers how to do routine work on their machines. The complicated procedures were made easier to understand through the use of comics. Eisner worked on *Preventative Maintenance* for 24 years before returning to the world of popular comics.

drafted: required to join the military.

WORDS TO KNOW

MAKE YOUR COMICS MAKE SENSE

Supplies: *pencils, paper, ruler, pens*

By combining words and pictures, you can make a superhero comic that packs a punch!

1 On scratch paper, draw thumbnails for your superhero comic. Make sure there are plenty of chances for action. Remember, your comic should have a beginning, middle, and end. Use as many panels as you need to tell your story.

2 While you sketch your thumbnail, include some words along with pictures. **Here are a few rules about including words in your comics.**

* Always have most of your words appear at the top of your panel

* Always write out your words BEFORE you draw your word balloons, thought clouds, and narrative boxes to make sure you have enough space.

* Avoid covering your characters with word balloons and thought clouds.

3 Try to include a different type of sound or way of communicating in your comic, such as telepathy, radio, a different language, or yelling.

4 Explore unique panel designs in your thumbnail. How can you use different panel shapes to show movement or emphasize the action?

5 Try adding some sound effects to your thumbnails. How will you make them look like different noises on the page?

6 Copy your thumbnails into your notebook. In the United States, we read left to right, top to bottom. Because of how we read, we need to lay out comic pages in same pattern. Check your comic to make sure your panel designs and sound effects make sense.

TRY THIS! Check out some comic books and **graphic novels** at your local library. As you read through them, pay attention to panel designs and how the cartoonist uses word balloons. Can you find any other rules? Do any of the cartoonists break the rules? Did it make sense to change or break the rules?

WORDS TO KNOW

graphic novel: a comic as long as a book, that tells one story.

MAKE A DYNAMIC COVER

Supplies: *pencils, paper, hero design, villain design, colored pencils or markers, rulers, digital camera, a few friends*

During the Golden Age, covers often made the difference between good sales and bad sales. Covers showed lots of action and the title was splashed across the top of the page. Words to help sell the comic were also placed in specific places.

1 Use a piece of scratch paper to do a few thumbnail drawings of your cover design. Think about where you want the title and how you want to show some action. Use stick figures to show the action between your hero and villain. Have your friends pose like the best design you come up with for the cover. Have one friend be the hero and the other be the villain. Take photos from a variety of angles until you find one you really like.

2 On a fresh sheet of paper, use a ruler to mark where the title and any other words will go. Use your photos as references to sketch out the action.

3 Once you are happy with the design, ink over everything with the pen. Then erase all the pencil marks. Now it's time to add color. You can photocopy your cover design if you want to be able to experiment with color before creating a final color version.

CHAPTER 4

INTO THE SILVER AGE OF COMICS

Silver Age: the era of comics between the introduction of the **Comics Code** in 1956 and the late 1970s.

Comics Code: a set of guidelines created by comics publishers to help regulate the content of comics.

WORDS TO KNOW

After World War II ended, America enjoyed the last of the Golden Age of comics before moving into what is known as the **Silver Age** of comics. Romance comics became popular, daily newspaper comic strips provided readers with the entertainment they wanted, and the photocopier was born during this era.

ROMANCE IN THE AIR

Americans grew tired of reading about heroes and villains after the war. Comic book publishers saw their sales falling and knew they needed to publish different work. Most created westerns or adventures, but a few publishers took a risk with romance.

WORDS TO KNOW

The first successful **romance comic** was *Archie*. Published by MLJ Magazines, the series was roughly based on the popular teenage movies of Mickey Rooney, and told the tale of the love life of Archie Andrews. Bob Montana was the cartoonist who brought *Archie* to life. The comic is still popular today and can be found in the magazine rack of almost any supermarket in the country!

ARCHIE EVENTUALLY BECAME SO POPULAR THAT MLJ MAGAZINES RENAMED ITS COMIC COMPANY ARCHIE COMICS.

Inspired by the success of *Archie*, other publishers quickly adopted the idea of romance comics. A very popular one called *Young Romance* came from an unlikely team—Joe Simon and Jack Kirby, the creators of *Captain America*.

OH, EUGENE! YOU REALLY KNOW HOW TO BE A BETTER BOYFRIEND THAN THAT QUARTERBACK.

DID YOU KNOW?

For a time in the 1950s, the best-selling comics were romance comics. The first printing of *Young Romance*, created by the same team as *Captain America*, sold 92 percent of its 500,000 copies.

Romance comics turned around the classic ideas of romance. Many of the stories put the female main character in charge of finding a boyfriend. She'd discover that the ugly duckling was the best boyfriend of all. The comic books challenged some of the long-held ideas Americans had about finding love and romance, that looks weren't everything and money didn't equal happiness.

DAILY COMICS

Meanwhile, the daily comic strips in newspapers were the envy of the comics world. The founders of the modern newspaper comic industry, Hearst and Pulitzer, developed a system called **syndication** that allowed comic strips to be sold to a variety of newspapers. King Features Syndicate, founded by Hearst, is still one of the leading comic strip syndicates in America. The syndicates were the business people between the cartoonists and the newspapers that published them.

WORDS TO KNOW

syndication: when the rights to print or broadcast a creative work are sold.

CARTOONISTS COULD FOCUS ON THEIR ART AND LET THE SYNDICATE HANDLE ALL THE BUSINESS.

Daily cartoonists had to work within the specific structure and size of each comic, unlike early cartoon masters who had whole pages. But in art, restrictions can lead to great creativity.

Al Capp created *Li'l Abner*, one of the most popular daily comic characters of the 1940s and '50s. The character of *Li'l Abner* was a strong, slow-witted, backwoods man who was accompanied by lots of different characters in the small Southern town of Dogpatch. One of those characters was the Shmoo.

The Shmoo were small, white, bowling pin–shaped creatures that quickly reproduced and were said to be the "tastiest critter" in the world. They were cute, lovable, laid eggs, and were easy to catch and cook. America loved the idea of the perfect animal and bought lots of Shmoo merchandise.

IN 1947, SHMOO PRODUCTS SOLD $25 MILLION WORTH OF STUFF—THAT'S EQUAL TO $257 MILLION TODAY!

DAGNAMMIT LI'L ABNER! I'M THE BOSS HERE AND YOU NEED TO GET TO WORKING HARDER TO MAKE ME MONEY, OR MY NAME AIN'T AL CAPP!

SOAP

Chester Gould created *Dick Tracy*. The main character was a detective who wore a bright yellow trench coat, used ultra-modern gadgets, and had plenty of helpers in his fight against organized crime.

Dick Tracy was drawn in a weird, **stylized** form with a range of bad guys whose names were associated with the way they looked. PruneFace was drawn as a face with so many wrinkles you couldn't make out his expression. Mumbles had an extremely small mouth. The strips always ended with a **cliffhanger**.

stylize: to draw comics in a specific way.
cliffhanger: an exciting moment that makes you wonder what happens next.

WORDS TO KNOW

Ohio cartoonist Milton "Milt" Caniff created two of the most popular adventure strips of the day: *Terry and the Pirates* and *Steve Canyon*. Caniff is famous for his realistic drawing style, and he loved to show as much action as he could get away with.

WORDS TO KNOW

serialize: to create a series of stories.

punch line: the sentence, statement, or phrase that makes the point, as in a joke.

Terry and the Pirates used cliffhangers to tease its audience into reading the next day's strip. Sometimes the stories in *Terry and the Pirates* and *Steve Canyon* were **serialized** over entire months! Can you think of a modern television series that uses cliffhangers to keep people watching week after week?

Blondie, created in 1933 by Murat "Chic" Young, was a daily comic about home, work, and relationships. The comic usually ended on a **punch line**. Blondie and her husband, Dagwood Bumstead, are still fixtures in the comics, though they're written and drawn by different cartoonists. *Blondie* was the most widely syndicated comic of its time, and it inspired many other daily comics, such as *Hi and Lois*, *For Better or For Worse*, and *The Family Circle*.

Compare a *Blondie* comic from 1933 with *Blondie* comics from today. Do they look different? Is the dialogue different? What are some of the reasons comics change over the decades? Cover up neighboring QR codes to make sure you're scanning the right one.

WHERE'S THE MONEY?

Often, the creators of newspaper comic strips were financially better off than their comic book counterparts. Harold Gray, creator of *Little Orphan Annie*, retired as a millionaire. The creators of *Superman*, on the other hand, accidently gave most of their rights to their publisher, DC Comics. Jerry Siegel and Joe Shuster were eventually replaced as the creative team for *Superman* and both lived the rest of their lives in near poverty.

Military humor was popular after the war. Mort Walker introduced the world to *Beetle Bailey* in 1950. The comic strip followed the Army life of a private at a military base and his run-ins with the overweight and often quick-tempered Sarge. Through the lens of humor, *Beetle Bailey* commented on social issues of the time, such as the war in Vietnam and the draft. *Beetle Bailey* is still enjoyed by daily newspaper readers today.

DID YOU KNOW?

It may seem as though a lot of movies based on comics have come out recently, but did you know the comic with the most movies is *Blondie*? Between 1938 and 1950, 28 full-length movies based on the daily strip were produced. That's more than any other comic, even *Batman*!

CHARLES SCHULZ AND *PEANUTS*

Have you ever read the *Peanuts* comic strip or seen one of the *Peanuts* television shows? You have Charles Schulz to thank. Schulz specialized in drawing children and came up with an idea for a daily comic strip called *Li'l Folks*. The syndicates he sent his *Li'l Folks* comics to didn't know what to think of them.

More *Peanuts!* PS

CHARLES SCHULZ'S COMIC STRIP WAS THE FIRST TO FEATURE ALL CHILDREN!

71

As an instructor in an art school, Charles Schulz was famous for holding contests to see who could draw the longest straight line without a ruler. **Watch him draw Charlie Brown!**

PS

Li'l Folks was populated entirely by children who often expressed very grown-up emotions. The star of the comic, Charlie Brown, constantly battled disappointment and depression. Finally, a syndicate agreed to give *Li'l Folks* a chance in 1950. They renamed it *Peanuts*, and it became one of the most famous comics in the world.

THE SIDEKICK CHARACTER IN *PEANUTS*, SNOOPY THE DOG, IS AS RECOGNIZABLE AS MICKEY MOUSE.

SCARY COMICS

As comic books in the late 1940s and early 1950s turned away from superheroes and toward romance, some comic publishers decided to tell darker stories. This may have seemed like a good idea, but those dark tales helped cause the end of the Golden Age. The covers often showed violent scenes to entice newsstand readers. Two comics were figureheads of this new trend in American comics—*Crime Does Not Pay* and EC Comics' *Tales from the Crypt.*

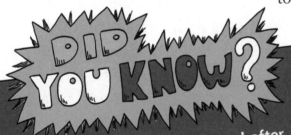

Unlike other strips that have continued after the original artist dies, Schulz did not want *Peanuts* to continue without him. *Peanuts* ended in 2000 and remains the longest-running comic strip written and drawn by the same cartoonist—50 years worth. That's more than 18,000 comic strips!

THE AMAZING XEROX MACHINE

Before the 1950s, making a copy of something took a lot of time and effort. If a business wanted to copy a document, it had to use carbon paper to make a **carbon copy**. Enter Chester Carlson, New York attorney and the inventor of the photocopier.

Tired of the long copying process, Carlson began to experiment in his kitchen with light-sensitive particles to print copies on paper. In 1938, he applied for a **patent**, but it wasn't until 1947 that a small company in New York decided to take a chance on his invention. The company called the process **xerography** and became the Xerox Corporation.

The photocopier was very important to the future of comics because it made the creation of **independent comics** cheaper and easier. It also played a big role in the birth of the modern graphic novel, but more on that in a later chapter.

The comic book *Crime Does Not Pay* was inspired by old police gazettes of the nineteenth century, which were often highly illustrated. The comic took the most shocking true news stories and illustrated them in comic form. It was one of the first to feature a master of ceremonies, or **emcee**. This character, called Mr. Crime, helped narrate the stories. The emcee character was used in most crime and horror comics of the era.

WORDS TO KNOW

carbon copy: an exact copy of a document made using carbon paper between two or more pieces of paper.

patent: a document from the government that gives an inventor the exclusive right to make, use, or sell his or her invention.

xerography: a way of making a copy using light-sensitive chemicals and paper.

independent comic: a comic book published without the help of a large company.

emcee: a master of ceremonies who helps to lead a story or event.

moral: a valuable lesson to help people know how to behave.

WORDS TO KNOW

REMEMBER, KIDS, CRIME DOESN'T PAY! BECAUSE...

I'M BROKE!

PARENTS WERE CONCERNED THAT THESE COMICS WERE BAD FOR KIDS, AND BEGAN TO PRESSURE PUBLISHERS AND THE GOVERNMENT FOR SOME RULES AND REGULATIONS.

Competing with *Crime Does Not Pay*, EC Comics became one of the most well-known publishers of crime, war, and horror comics in America. EC published *Tales from the Crypt*, which featured a rotating cast of emcees. The comic told graphic horror stories with twist endings and **morals**. The covers were gruesome and brightly colored, like the pulp magazines of the early part of the twentieth century.

American adults loved their crime and horror comics. Unfortunately, newsstands mixed all of the comic books together. A kid who wanted to read the latest *Scrooge McDuck* comic might pick up an issue of *Crime Does Not Pay* out of curiosity.

DID YOU KNOW?

Tales from the Crypt and other comics from EC Comics inspired a young Stephen King, who grew up and wrote scary stories.

THE END OF THE GOLDEN AGE

Have you ever heard people say that videogames containing violence can make kids violent? People used to say the same thing about comics!

Concern over comics kept growing in the early 1950s. People even burned comic books in protest. In 1954, a psychologist named Dr. Fredric Wertham published a book called *Seduction of the Innocent*, which argued that children who can't tell fiction from reality get confused by comic books. He claimed that comic books lead to violent behavior.

Due to Wertham's book and public pressure, the U.S. Senate decided to hold **hearings** on the negative effects of comics. The Senate called Bill Gaines, the publisher for EC Comics, to the stand.

Before he entered the Senate building, Gaines took some medication that his doctor had prescribed to help his nerves. That was a mistake! The drugs made him confused. By the end of his testimony, he had agreed that the comics he created were completely inappropriate.

hearing: a special session of Congress or the Senate held to "hear" from witnesses and experts on a given issue.

WORDS TO KNOW

THE AMERICAN PUBLIC WAS FURIOUS.

75

Comic publishers feared the government would **censor** their work. Gaines gathered the major comic publishers together to figure out a plan to get Americans to trust comic books again. They formed the Comics Magazine Association of America (CMAA) and elected the publisher of Archie Comics as president. They created a set of rules called the Comics Code. All comics that followed these rules were given a special CMAA badge to print on the covers of their comics.

censor: to examine books, movies, letters, etc., in order to remove things that are considered to be offensive or harmful to society.

WORDS TO KNOW

OH NO! IT'S THE WICKED COTTON CANDY KING! GOOD THING I BROUGHT MY BATBRUSH!

The Comics Code was the end of publishers such as EC Comics and *Crime Does Not Pay*. Superheroes couldn't be shown fighting bad guys with guns, so action scenes and weapons became silly. Comics historians call this era the Silver Age.

BAH! I WILL GET YOU WITH MY CAVITY RAY!

As comics became more and more goofy in the 1960s and '70s, adults moved away from reading comics. Comic creators needed superheroes for a younger audience. A young man named Steve Ditko joined the Marvel Comics team with the idea for a teenager with the powers of a spider. The result was *The Amazing Spider-Man*.

TEAM SUPER

During the Senate hearings of 1954, many publishers had to sell their characters to keep from going out of business. DC Comics, publisher of *Batman* and *Superman*, bought several new heroes, and then faced the problem of mixing them in with its old heroes. In the early 1960s, DC Comics launched the solution—the superhero team.

The *Justice League of America (JLA)* joined up the heroes of DC Comics to overcome galactic bad guys. The *JLA* had memorable members such as Batman, Superman, and Wonder Woman, but also included newly bought heroes, such as The Flash, Green Lantern, and the Martian Manhunter.

Until the 1960s, Marvel Comics was known for copying the popular comics of the day, from romance to westerns to giant monster comics. When Jack Kirby returned from the war and from making romance comics, he and the editor-in-chief, Stan "Lee" Lieber, came up with the idea of a team of scientists who were changed into superheroes by cosmic rays. The team was called the Fantastic Four.

Fans immediately flocked to Marvel Comics. The good news was Stan Lee and Jack Kirby were just getting started. In the following years, the duo created almost all of what would become known as the Marvel Superheroes. Together they introduced the Hulk, Iron Man, the X-Men, Thor, and another super team that brought back a hero from the Golden Age—Captain America.

Jack Kirby had the idea of bringing Captain America, who had been lost in the North Sea after World War II, back from the 1940s. Stan Lee loved the idea, and together they came up with the *Avengers*. The comic was a hit.

THROUGHOUT THE HISTORY OF MARVEL COMICS, ALMOST ALL OF MARVEL'S HEROES HAD TURNS AT BEING AN AVENGER.

JAM COMICS

Supplies: *pencils, paper, pens, friends*

Comics don't need to be a lonely art. Drawing a comic with friends can be a fun and funny time! Jam comics are a perfect way to have fun with a group.

1 Sit in a circle. Give each person a sheet of paper and a pencil or pen. Have everyone write a title and draw a panel at the top of the page. The first panel should show a character or two and set up an action.

2 Pass the page to the right. Don't say anything about your drawing. All the information the person to your right needs will be in your title and first panel.

3 Read the comic you got from the person on your left. Draw a new panel and add your spin on the story.

4 Repeat steps two and three until everyone has drawn a panel on each comic. Pass the comics back to their original creators and read the stories everyone created. Are they different from what the first person intended? Are they funny?

TRY THIS! Some cartoonists like to create pages and pages of jam comics around a theme or story. How could you make a jam comic book with your friends? What themes or ideas would you use?

MAKE A DAILY COMIC STRIP

Supplies: *notebook with un-ruled paper (a new manga sketchbook would work well), scratch paper, pencil, pen, small ruler*

A daily comic is a fun, quick way to practice making comics. They don't need to be funny and they could even be about your own life! A lot of cartoonists do a daily comic strip, even if they never publish them.

1 Choose a theme. What will your daily strip be about? Do you want it to be funny or dramatic? About your daily life? Will it have a changing cast of characters? What about the title?

2 Choose a daily design. If you choose to make a one-panel gag comic, what shape is your single panel going to be? If you do a strip, how many panels will you use each day?

3 Creating a daily comic can be a lot of work. It might be helpful to brainstorm a bunch of comic ideas ahead and map them on a calendar.

4 Now it's time to put all your new cartooning skills to work. First, make thumbnail sketches, then pencil, ink, and color your comic strip. Create a new one every day!

USE THE "MARVEL METHOD"

Supplies: *friends who each take one job (writer, penciler, inker, colorist), art supplies for each job*

Inspired by Henry Ford's assembly line system of manufacturing, Marvel Comics decided to try a new way of making comics that would streamline the process. This became known as the <u>Marvel Method</u>. Get together with your friends and follow the Marvel Method to create a comic!

1 **WRITER:** First, the writer comes up with a plot for the story. For example, Super Mole saves his family from the clutches of Grumpy Gardener with his powers of super digging. The writer also gives information about other characters, how the story should be told, and anything else he or she thinks the penciler should know.

2 **PENCILER:** The penciler uses the plot and character notes from the writer and makes thumbnails to visually tell the story. He or she then carefully pencils the action for each panel. The penciler doesn't write out any words, but leaves room for the writer to add them in the next step.

Marvel Method: a way of creating comics that relies on an assembly-line format.

3 **WRITER:** The writer adds narration blocks, word balloons, and thought clouds to match the action and panels.

WORDS TO KNOW

4 **INKER:** The inker traces over the important lines from the penciler and the writer. The inker might also make slight changes to the art, such as adding sound effects, defining shadows, and drawing dark lines to add complexity to each panel. Once finished, the inker erases any pencil lines and the comic goes to the colorist.

5 **COLORIST:** The colorist chooses colors for the comic and makes the comic come alive.

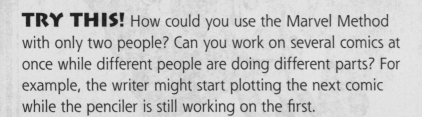

TRY THIS! How could you use the Marvel Method with only two people? Can you work on several comics at once while different people are doing different parts? For example, the writer might start plotting the next comic while the penciler is still working on the first.

THE MARVEL METHOD

Stan Lee and Jack Kirby came up with the Marvel Method for their first *Fantastic Four* comic. Here's how it worked. Stan came up with a plot for the comic and gave the idea to an artist, who drew the whole comic out, telling the story visually. Then Stan added narration and dialogue to the pages. The Marvel Method allowed for a freer visual style, and the artists were able to tell the stories how they envisioned them. Before the Marvel Method, writers completely scripted out the whole comic, including what the panels would look like.

MAKE A SUPERHERO TEAM

PROJECT!

Supplies: *pencils, paper, colored pencils*

Marvel and DC realized the popularity of superhero teams in the 1950s. What makes these teams so much fun?

> CREATING YOUR OWN SUPER TEAM CAN TAKE SOME TIME, BUT THE MAIN THING YOU HAVE TO REMEMBER IS BALANCE!

1 Brainstorm some ideas on a piece of paper. What would a superhero team's job be? Why are they a team? What sort of name would fit the team? How are they related to each other? What brought them together?

2 Draw your team, give each member of the team a name, and show his or her power. What makes a good team? If they all had the same type of powers, they wouldn't be very interesting. What kind of abilities do you want on your team? What powers should they have?

3 Try designing costumes that are unique to each character, but still make them look like they belong to a team.

4 Lastly, design a secret home base for your team. For example, the Justice League of America meets in an orbiting space station. What and where will your superhero team call home base?

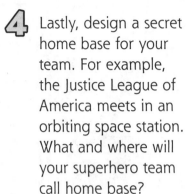

DID YOU KNOW?

Teams are everywhere in the world of comics! The X-Men are all students with mutant super powers, the Incredibles are a family, the Fantastic Four are scientists, and the Guardians of the Galaxy are a galactic police team. They each have jobs based around who they are and what they should be doing.

LET'S FIGHT THESE BAD GUYS AND MEET BACK AT TUNNEL COVE FOR ICE CREAM!

PS

The 1960s saw the start of a popular television show based on the comic book hero Batman. It came out shortly after the invention of color television and featured extremely bright colors, crazy costumes, and silly language. The star of the show, Adam West, played Batman and his alter ego, Bruce Wayne, in a deliberately silly way. **Watch the introduction credits to the 1960s *Batman* television show.** Does the theme song sound familiar? How are the graphics different from television shows today?

CHAPTER 5

LIFE AFTER THE COMICS CODE

Not every comics artist wanted to follow the rules of the Comics Code from the 1950s. Many wanted to explore serious subjects, and they wanted to take plenty of space to do it. Some comics artists began to produce and distribute their own comic books. With help from the Xerox machine, they could cheaply print lots of copies of their independent comics. The longer independent comics were called graphic novels.

INDEPENDENCE!

Imagine having someone tell you what your comics have to be about every time you sit down to draw. Does that like fun? Many comic book artists in the 1960s through the 1980s wanted to be able to express their creativity without worrying about the Comics Code. A few brave artists decided to do just that.

Larry Marder began publishing his comic, *Tales of the Beanworld*, in 1980. He was first inspired by the story his mother tells of how his head looked like a bean when he was born. In college he started drawing little bean-shaped characters that eventually became the cast of his comic.

mythology: a set of stories or beliefs about a particular religion or culture.

WORDS TO KNOW

As his comic evolved, Marder explored themes found within **mythology** and Native American cultures. His characters live in a place called Beanworld. What do you think Marder means when he says, "Beanworld isn't a place, it's a process?"

In 1984, two friends from Massachusetts published the first edition of a comic that would become an international, multi-million-dollar phenomenon. *Teenage Mutant Ninja Turtles* (*TMNT*) was created by Peter Laird and Kevin Eastman. Originally meant to be a joke about an absurd jumble of words, the comic was instantly popular among comic book fans. The two started their own publishing company, Mirage Studios, to publish the book.

OK, OK... SO... THESE, TURTLES ARE... UH, LIKE THESE SEWER-DWELLING NINJAS!

YEAH! YEAH! AND THEY COULD BE MUTANTS FROM THIS OOZE... AND THEY'RE TEENAGERS!

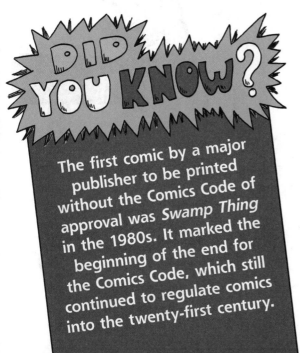

DID YOU KNOW?

The first comic by a major publisher to be printed without the Comics Code of approval was *Swamp Thing* in the 1980s. It marked the beginning of the end for the Comics Code, which still continued to regulate comics into the twenty-first century.

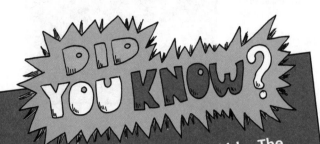

At first, TMNT wasn't for kids. The turtles used adult language and plenty of violence when fighting bad guys. When TMNT became a children's animated television show in 1987, the television turtles behaved much better. The comic book turtles, however, still continued to be published for an older audience.

direct mail: a system used to sell things directly to subscribers through the U.S. mail.
zine: a self-published magazine, usually produced using photocopiers.

WORDS TO KNOW

TMNT made hundreds of millions of dollars for their creators through action figures, four feature-length movies, several video games, and two follow-up cartoon shows. Laird and Eastman remained true to their independent comics roots and founded the Xeric Grant to help support other independent cartoonists.

One reason independent comics were so successful was the **direct mail** system. Up until the late 1970s, comics could only be purchased at newsstands, drug stores, and supermarkets. New companies began to form to distribute comics to readers through the mail. Readers just needed to get a catalog from a distributor to order the comics they wanted.

OH!!! I HOPE MY COMICS CAME TODAY!

THANKS TO THE XEROX COPIER AND DIRECT MAIL, SELF-PUBLISHED MAGAZINES CALLED zines (PRONOUNCED "ZEENS") COULD BE CREATED QUICKLY AND CHEAPLY, THEN SENT TO READERS.

Early writers of zines, who called themselves **zinesters**, created zines about everything from politics to rock bands. Zines were often quickly made and easily sold or traded with other zine creators. It was a way to bypass the often difficult-to-enter publishing world.

zinester: a person who makes zines.

mini comic: a small, self-published comic.

parody: an imitation of something for comical effect.

WORDS TO KNOW

> **BEFORE THE INTERNET, ZINES WERE THE CHEAPEST AND MOST EFFECTIVE WAY OF GETTING YOUR STORY READ BY AN AUDIENCE.**

MINI COMICS! WHAT A GREAT CONCEPT!

Mini comics developed out of the independent zines of the 1980s. These self-published comics are very small, which make them easy to produce and distribute. A comics artist will often begin his or her career creating and selling mini comics until a publisher discovers him or her.

LOOOOONG COMICS

Many independent comic book creators collected their comics into thick paperback books to be sold in bookstores. Today, we know them as graphic novels and they are still very popular.

One of the first graphic novels was written in the 1970s. Canadian cartoonist Dave Sim drew a **parody** of other comics about magic and barbarians. He called it *Cerebus* after the title character, a barbarian warrior aardvark. Originally meant to be humorous, the comic grew into something bigger. Sim started to tell long stories in his comic about everything from religion to politics.

Sim wrote the comic and drew the characters, but hired another artist to draw all of the background art. When a storyline was completed, Sim bundled the issues together in a thick, phonebook-shaped package to sell. These collections are some of the first examples of the modern graphic novel. Together, they created one of the largest collected independent comics of all time—more than 6,000 pages long!

Another successful, long independent comic book from the late 1970s came from the husband-and-wife team of Richard and Wendy Pini. Their comic book was called *Elfquest*. The first issue appeared in a **fantasy** comic magazine called *Fantasy Quarterly* in 1977.

WORDS TO KNOW

fantasy: a **genre** of comics and literature based on myth and legend.

genre: a type of creative work, such as mystery, romance, or fantasy.

WHATCHA' CALL IT?

The term graphic novel became widely used when Will Eisner finished his work for the U.S. Army and returned to making comic books. He thought of a new way to present his comics to the world—not through a printed monthly comic book, but through a published, hardcover book sold in bookstores. The books were popular, and people started to take comics seriously again as an art form.

MR. EISNER! MAN, THIS IS HUGE!!! LIKE A REAL COMIC BOOK!

WELL, I LIKE TO THINK OF IT AS A GRAPHIC NOVEL.

Some graphic novel artists found inspiration in very serious stories. Would you want to read a comic book about the **Holocaust**?

Art Spiegelman's father was a survivor of Auschwitz, one of the most horrible Nazi **concentration camps**. Spiegelman decided to tell his story using animals as the characters. In his graphic novel, *Maus*, Jews were mice and Nazis were cats. He hoped that this technique would make the hard topic easier for readers to look at. He could show disturbing scenes without having to draw the suffering faces of real people.

DID YOU KNOW?

Graphic novels can be about anything and for anyone. Art Spiegelman and his wife, Francoise Mouly, publish a children's graphic novel series called *Little Lit*, which takes classic <u>folk tales</u> and retells them for kids!

THESE BOOKS WERE DIFFICULT TO MAKE, SINCE THEY WERE VERY REAL TO ME.

I LIKE TO THINK THEY MADE A DIFFERENCE, THOUGH.

MAUS WAS COLLECTED INTO A TWO-VOLUME GRAPHIC NOVEL IN 1991 AND BECAME THE FIRST COMIC TO WIN THE Pulitzer Prize FOR LITERATURE.

WORDS TO KNOW

Holocaust: a time before and during World War II when the German Nazis tried to kill the entire Jewish race, as well as several other groups.

concentration camp: a prison where people were sent during the Holocaust to be killed or made to do hard work.

folk tale: a story told by a specific group of people, often involving magic and a moral.

Pulitzer Prize: a group of prizes awarded annually for work done in journalism, fiction, and non-fiction, as well as for photojournalism.

INDIE GRAPHIC NOVEL PUBLISHERS

Many of the new graphic novels were being published by small independent companies. The three major publishers were Top Shelf, Fantagraphics, and the Canadian publisher, Drawn and Quarterly.

THEY WERE INDEPENDENT BECAUSE THEY WERE NOT OWNED OR OPERATED BY ANY OF THE MAIN PUBLISHING COMPANIES OF THE DAY.

imprint: a part of a publishing company that publishes a certain type of book.

WORDS TO KNOW

The work of these publishers helped change the perception of comics in America. Their graphic novels were more serious. As book critics and readers began to take note of the more mature work, major book publishers were inspired to start their own graphic novel **imprints**.

The first major publisher to enter the field was Pantheon Press, the publisher for Art Spiegelman. Pantheon could get graphic novels into major bookstores. In the mid-1990s, the comic book sections of bookstores were made up of mostly superhero comics with a few graphic novels sprinkled in. By the early 2000s, the comics section was renamed the graphic novel section and began to take up whole rows of shelves.

DID YOU KNOW?

In 2006, major publisher Harcourt Press created an imprint called Hill and Wang to publish serious graphic novels. It produces biographies of presidents, histories of literature movements, and graphic novels about science. If you ever see a graphic novel about history or science, check the publisher. Is it published by Hill and Wang?

IMAGE COMICS

The late 1980s and early 1990s saw some of Marvel Comics's biggest sales, thanks to the artistic talent of its comic creators. These artists worked hard to produce the best superhero comics possible. However, most of the comics created by DC and Marvel were owned by the companies, not by the writers and artists. This meant the money from sales of comics, T-shirts, or movies went to the company. Some of the artists wanted more creative say and control over their characters.

In 1992, several artists and writers, mostly from Marvel, decided to quit working for the big publishers and start their own company. The result was Image Comics. It began with a simple idea: that the creators of comics should retain complete control over their characters and comic book stories.

The first comics to be published by Image were very successful. As the popularity of Image Comics grew, more comics artists joined Image to publish their own comics. Today, it remains one of the most successful independent comic book publishers and often is considered a mainstream comics publisher.

IMAGE REFUSED TO JOIN THE COMICS CODE AUTHORITY, WHICH MEANS THAT ITS COMICS CAN'T BE CENSORED BY ANYONE OUTSIDE OF ITS OWN OFFICES.

91

THE COMIC BOOKSTORE

As comic books and graphic novels started to become popular again, they needed a place where fans could find them. Comic bookstores popped up all across America during the 1980s and mid-1990s. People who loved comics could browse shelves stocked with books, T-shirts, action figures, and posters. They could even write a list of their favorite comic titles, and when the bookstore got a shipment, the employees would pull those titles aside and save them. This was called a **pull list**. Most big towns still have one or two comic stores and you can still make a "pull" of your favorite comics. Check them out sometime—you might even make some new friends who love the same comics as you!

pull list: a list of comics that your local comic bookstore will order and set aside for you.

WORDS TO KNOW

NEWSPAPER COMICS IN THE MODERN AGE

Independent comics creators and publishers weren't the only ones enjoying the modern age of comics. Newspaper comics also thrived between the late 1970s and 1990s.

These newspaper comics had changed through the decades. When Charles Schulz introduced *Peanuts* in 1950, his use of a simple background was new and innovative. In the '70s, '80s, and '90s, most comic strips relied more on memorable characters than complicated settings to stay popular.

If someone was to ask you the name of the fat orange cat who loves lasagna, you'd probably shout, "Garfield!" In the 1970s, Jim Davis created a strip that mostly took place on the floor or countertop, with very few extra details. The humans in the strip interacted with Garfield, but they couldn't hear what Garfield was thinking. However, the audience knew Garfield's thoughts, through the use of a thought cloud.

GARFIELD WAS A commercial SUCCESS! HE IS STILL FOUND ON EVERYTHING FROM COFFEE MUGS TO T-SHIRTS AND IS AN ANIMATED TV SERIES.

commercial: operating as a business to earn money.

WORDS TO KNOW

HE MAY BE A LAZY CAT, BUT WE'VE DONE SOME GREAT WORK.

...ZZZ...

Not every cartoonist was interested in commercial success. In 1985, Bill Watterson introduced the world to a boy and a stuffed tiger in what many consider to be one of the top 10 comic strips of all time. People ages 6 to 96 love *Calvin and Hobbes*. No other comic strip has been so popular with such a wide range of ages.

Watterson says he was inspired partly by his own childhood and partly by the comic strip greats who came before him. These include Winsor McCay, George Herriman, Walt Kelly, and Charles Schulz.

More *Garfield*!

Bill Watterson gave a speech at Kenyon College in 1990 that was made into a cartoon by comics artist Gavin Aung Than. Can you find similarities between Than's comic and Watterson's style of drawing?

PS

93

Plans were made for *Calvin and Hobbes* to appear on everything from socks to hats and there was even talk of a television series, but Bill Watterson said no. He wanted his strip to be enjoyed as a comic strip and nothing more. He successfully fought against marketing his strip on other products, something comics had been doing since *The Yellow Kid* almost 100 years before. Even after he retired *Calvin and Hobbes* in 1995, he still refused to allow his characters to be used in other places.

DID YOU KNOW?

You may have seen window decals on cars of Calvin peeing on another logo. These stickers are not technically legal. Bill Watterson neither designed them nor sees any money from their sales.

More *Calvin and Hobbes*! **PS**

MANGA

Let's take a moment and travel to Japan! Remember Hokusai, who invented manga? Cartooning was popular in Japan through the early twentieth century. After World War II, the Japanese comics from before the war were associated with the empire, which had fallen. No one wanted to read these comics anymore. The manga that took its place after the war became the most popular form of comics in the world.

Manga publishers sprang up all across the country. They printed their comics in quarterly, monthly, and even weekly editions. Manga books were the size of telephone books.

MANGA STORIES WERE ABOUT EVERYTHING, FROM LIFE AS AN OFFICE WORKER TO BEING A SPACE EXPLORER.

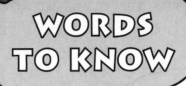

anime: Japanese animation.

WORDS TO KNOW

The biggest name in manga grew to fame in the late '40s and early '50s. Osamu Tezuka was inspired by the comics and cartoons he saw from America, such as Walt Disney's work. Tezuka chose to focus his early comics on a general audience and grew a large following of fans. His first **anime**, which is a form of manga-style animation, was called *Astro Boy*. It was one of the first Japanese comics to be seen by Americans. During the course of his career, Tezuka wrote and drew more than 150,000 pages of comics, as well as directed several animated features and series of his work.

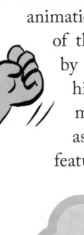

OSAMU TEZUKA IS OFTEN CALLED THE WALT DISNEY OF JAPAN.

MANGA AND ANIME

Many Americans first experienced Japan's comic style in the form of anime. Often people confuse anime and manga. Many of the manga that Tezuka created for print were then made into anime. Other times, the anime would inspire a printed run of manga. A good rule of thumb when you see Japanese cartooning is if it moves, it's anime. If it doesn't, it's manga!

When manga became popular in America, the language translation was the easy part. The structure of the comic was harder. The Japanese read from right to left, which means their front covers are our back covers. In order for Americans to read them from left to right, the pages and panels had to be rearranged!

I JUST LOVE TO READ MANGA!

American readers at first didn't understand certain expressions and gestures of manga characters, but it didn't take long before people loved reading them. Today, American publishers no longer switch the layout of manga books. American readers are used to reading them from right to left, just like the Japanese!

ALTHOUGH I HAD TO GET USED TO READING FROM RIGHT TO LEFT!

Manga

COMIC-CON!

Comic book lovers often gather at **conventions** called Comic-Con. The Golden State Comic-Con was the first, in 1970 with 300 attendees. By 1980, it had been renamed the San Diego Comic-Con and more than 5,000 people went. Today, more than 100,000 people visit every year! Comic-Cons are held all over the world. Anyone can buy table space to sell his or her comics. Some of the best-known conventions are Stumptown, SPX, APE, and MoCCA. People even go dressed as their favorite characters!

convention: a gathering of people who are all interested in a certain idea, topic, or event.

WORDS TO KNOW

COSTUME FOR A COMIC-CON

Supplies: *images of the character you want to dress as, paper and pencil, supplies for gadgets (such as recycled boxes, plastic cans, and wrapping paper tubes), fabric, scissors, glue, paint, used clothing*

Many convention goers dress as their favorite characters. It's called cosplay, and it's a way to make conventions more fun.

1 Sketch out your costume. Use pictures of your character as a reference to sketch out what you need to make yourself look like the character.

2 Figure out what supplies you need to make each part of the costume. Can you get clothes at a used clothing store for your costume? These clothes can be cut up or painted and glued. Check the recycle bin for things such as cardboard and plastic.

3 Using your sketch as a guide, begin making the different parts of your costume. Ask an adult for help if you need it. Make sure to try on all the parts as you make them.

4 Be awesome. Wear your cool costume to a local comic convention. How many people knew who you were? How many other cosplayers did you meet? What kinds of tips did they share with you about making costumes?

TRY THIS! Gather a group of friends together to design costumes for a super team. Often, conventions have contests for the best group cosplay. See if you can win!

DRAW MANGA-STYLE CHARACTERS

Supplies: *pencils, pens, paper*

Comics look different in each part of the world. European comics often have a more sketchy style, while American comics have cleaner lines. Let's look at how to draw Japanese manga characters before we do the harder work of learning how to draw their faces!

1 Manga characters tend to have thin bodies, with long arms and legs. Start by drawing an action line for your character. Draw a larger-than-normal circle at the top for the head and then draw a thin rectangle for the body. Draw the sketchy skeleton for the arms and legs the same way you would for any other comic.

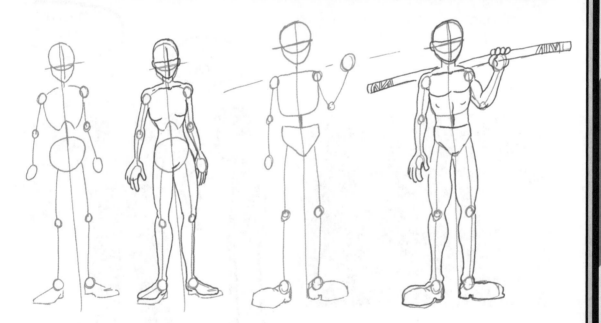

2 Add meat to the skeleton, but not too much! Often, manga characters have more slender arms and legs than American characters. This allows for the great expressive poses that manga is known for.

3 Add clothes and ink your manga character. Erase the pencil lines and add color!

TRY THIS! Can you turn your hero and villain characters into manga?

TRY THIS, TOO! In manga, a certain type of character drawing is known as the chibi. A chibi is a shortened version of the main character and it often looks like a child. Chibi are used to show extreme emotions and for **comic relief**. Look at the step-by-step illustrations shown here. Can you turn your manga character into a chibi?

DRAW MANGA-STYLE FACES

Supplies: *pencils, paper, pens*

The design of the faces is what makes manga so recognizable. Let's crack the code of what makes a face manga.

1 Unlike the oval face shapes of American comics, the general shape of a manga face is a large circle. Draw a circular face shape.

2 Just as in American comics, draw a vertical guideline down the middle of the face where the nose will go.

3 Unlike American comics, the horizontal line doesn't go through the middle of the face shape. Instead, it should go about two-thirds down from the top of the head. This is to give enough room for the large, iconic manga eyes.

4 Extend your vertical guideline through the bottom of the circle. Add the jawline and chin by connecting the bottom of the vertical guideline with the right and left ends of the horizontal guideline as shown in the example.

5 Manga noses are either very small or hugely expressive. Using the examples shown here, draw a nose between the horizontal guideline and the bottom of the circle.

6 Now draw the eyes following the step-by-step example shown below.

7 Draw the mouth, eyebrows, and ears. The mouth will be smaller than the eye guides. Look at the examples of manga mouths. The eyebrows, aren't much different from American eyebrows, and manga ears are either big or small, depending on your style.

8 Manga hair is super fun to draw since it can be really wild. Most manga women have long, flowing hair, which can be bunched up, braided, or swirling all around them. Manga men, and women, also often have angular, spiky hair. Open up any manga from your local library to see these different styles. Remember to make sure the hair is connected to the head.

TRY THIS! Try to draw yourself and people you know as manga characters. Is it easier or more difficult than trying to draw them as American cartoons?

MAP A LONG COMIC

Supplies: *ruled notebook, sketchbook, trusty pen or pencil*

Writing your own graphic novel will take time. It took Art Spiegelman more than 10 years to finish *Maus*! You can get started on your own graphic novel by laying the foundation with thumbnails and a script.

1 In your notebook, write a short paragraph describing what your graphic novel will be about. Will it be about space exploration? The Wild West? A historical event or past experience?

2 Break down your story. Start with three parts: beginning, middle, and end. Write a little about what happens in each part. Now break each part into sections, or scenes. Write a few words for each scene to tell what is happening.

3 Write a script. The script simply tells you what is going to happen on each page. Use your outline and write out what happens, section by section. Make sure you include some talking and notes for the actions. Break your script up into different comics pages as you go.

4 Using your script, thumbnail out what each page will look like in your sketchbook. Make changes. Every cartoonist always makes changes to his or her script and thumbnails as the graphic novel develops. Don't be afraid to change something if you have a cooler idea. That's all part of the process.

Page 1   Page 2   Page 3

CHAPTER 6

COMICS AND THE INTERNET

Comics artists often use the latest technology to create and publish their work. The most amazing technological advancement for comics has been the Internet. It was originally created by the U.S. military in the 1960s as a way to share information in case of a nuclear attack. But the Internet was only used by a few government agencies and universities through the 1970s.

The Internet's early design and coding was almost all done through experimentation and **collaboration** across several scientific and computer science communities. By the late 1980s, the Internet had evolved dramatically. While the first computers were the size of your garage, personal computers in the late 1980s were so small they could fit easily on your desk in the living room. The Internet is still changing today!

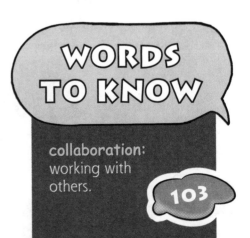

WORDS TO KNOW

collaboration: working with others.

103

Comics have come a long way from the big splashy pages of Hearst's and Pulitzer's newspapers. And comics are not just for kids anymore. Thanks to cheaper, high-quality printing technology, tablet devices, and the Internet, comics are finding new audiences all over the world.

WEBCOMICS

With the spread of the Internet, many cartoonists found that they could reach a wide audience without needing a publisher, comic syndicate, or even a printer. These early pioneers set their sites (pun intended) on cyberspace and boldly went where no cartoonist had gone before—online. Many of the first **webcomics** were quickly drawn stories about video game culture or humor revolving around a simple theme.

As the Internet became more a part of daily life, cartoonists used it to find an audience by establishing their own websites. There are also many comics apps that showcase the work of regular cartoonists and webcomics artists.

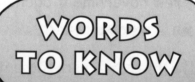

WORDS TO KNOW

webcomic: a comic made to be read on web browsers.

Here are some fun webcomics to find online, with your parents' permission, *The Last of the Polar Bears* by Lindsay Cibos and *Little Dee* by Chris Baldwin. How do the characters change through time? Do the stories make surprise twists? Cover up neighboring QR codes to make sure you're scanning the right one.

The advent of color printing and mass newspaper production technology before the turn of the twentieth century changed the world of comics. Today, new technologies of the twenty-first century drive innovations in comics and cartooning in much the same way.

The same technology that made the boom in webcomics possible has also reshaped the mini comics and indie comics world. Comics artists use laptops, digital scanners, and electronic drawing devices such as the **Wacom tablet** to edit and lay out their comics for print from their desks. Powerful **desktop publishing** software has given independent cartoonists new ways of making their art. The cost of printing or photocopying comics has also fallen, creating a perfect environment for self-publishing.

DID YOU KNOW?

When the Internet was first invented, electronic messaging was one of its first functions. One of the first messages to be sent over the Internet was about *Star Trek*, the new television show about space exploration. From the very beginning, people have been using the Internet to communicate about stuff they love!

WORDS TO KNOW

Wacom tablet: a device that allows an artist to draw life-like lines right onto a computer.

desktop publishing: computer software that edits and formats comics, books, and magazines.

COMIC BOOK CONNECTION

All new comic strip cartoonists rely on social media to connect with their audiences. They love to hear from their readers! Ask an adult for permission to follow the Twitter or Tumblr feeds of some of your favorite cartoonists.

screen print: to make a color print of an image with special ink pressed through screens.

WORDS TO KNOW

As more cartoonists learned to design their own comics using the latest computer technology, a flood of new talent poured into conventions such as SPX in Bethesda, Maryland, and APE in San Francisco. Independent mini comics and publishing conventions sprouted up across the nation in the mid-to-late 1990s.

Independent cartoonists found an audience eager to read something handmade in a world that has become very digital. Cartoonists created handmade **screen print** art on the covers of their mini comics, which gave each issue the look of having been crafted with care.

WANT ONE OF MY MINI COMICS?

YEAH! LET ME GET YOU ONE OF MINE.

IF YOU MAKE YOUR OWN MINI COMICS, TAKE THEM TO A MINI COMIC CONVENTION AND TRADE WITH OTHER CARTOONISTS.

THE FADING NEWSPAPER STRIPS

After staying popular for almost 100 years, national newspapers began to see a fall in the number of readers in the 1990s. With the rise of the Internet and the popularity of cable news channels, fewer people read newspapers to find out what is happening in the world. Do you still read newspapers?

Local newspaper companies began buying each other up to gain more readers, until only one or two local newspapers were left in most regions. The lack of competition meant that the comic syndicates couldn't find as many homes for their comic strips.

Comic syndicates also couldn't pay new cartoonists the kinds of salaries they offered in the 1960s and '70s. Now, each syndicate only accepts one or two new cartoonists a year, even though it usually receives about 5,000 submissions.

THESE NEW CARTOONISTS GET PAID VERY LITTLE. IT'S A VERY DIFFERENT JOB THAN IT WAS 50 YEARS AGO.

PUBLISHERS IN THE INTERNET AGE

How have comic book publishers adapted to the new world of the Internet? DC and Marvel began experimenting with new media in the late 1990s to try to get comics to fans in new ways. Today, their comics can be bought digitally, read digitally, and stored on a fan's device.

Both companies continue to try to find new ways to stay ahead of the technological curve. Meanwhile, print sales continue to decline. Maybe in a few years, major comic books such as *Superman* and *X-Men* will only be available as digital downloads.

At one of the first San Diego Comic-Cons, legendary cartoonist Jack Kirby said that in a few decades, Hollywood studios would be coming to the comic convention to look for the next big idea for a blockbuster film. He was right! From 2000 to 2013, a comic book movie has been one of the top-grossing films each year.

A few newspaper comic strips have thrived in spite of the Internet and television. *Pearls Before Swine* follows the example of *Garfield*. The characters often interact in a very spare environment, usually just a table and chairs, and rely on a punch line. *Rhymes with Orange* by Hilary Price is mostly a single-panel gag comic that combines social observation with bizarre humor. The comics page also now includes its first Latin American comic strip, called *Baldo*.

Perhaps the most popular new comic strip of this era is *Get Fuzzy*, a strip about a cat, a dog, and their human. Comic strips about talking animals have always been popular, but *Get Fuzzy*, drawn by Darby Conley, is one of the first to portray the cat and dog characters in an almost realistic style. *Get Fuzzy* embraces the more artful style of Bill Watterson.

What's next for comics? It's impossible to know! But we can guess that comics are here to stay, even if the way we produce and read them changes through time.

NEWSPAPERS ARE THE BEST PLACE FOR A COMIC.

Find more of these comics.

Cover up neighboring QR codes to make sure you're scanning the right one.

DESIGN YOUR TABLE FOR COMICS CONVENTIONS

Supplies: *banner paper, glue, glitter, paint, scissors, streamers, shoeboxes, cardboard, anything else you can think of to make things for your table*

Whether you decide to be a mini comics creator, a zinester, a graphic novelist, or a webcomics genius, one day you may want a table at a comic convention. Either by yourself or with friends, start to think about how you will design your table.

1 Decide on your table size. Most conventions will let you buy space at a whole table or a half table that you share with another cartoonist or artist. Once you know how much room you have, you can design what you need to stand out.

2 Use big sheets of paper to design a banner with the name of your comic or publishing group on it. You can paint original art on the banner or have your name in big glittery letters. Some comics artists like to hang a string in front of their banners for some sample comics.

3 Make a display stand for your comics. You can use shoe or cereal boxes for this step. People love to see comics standing upright so they can get a good look at the covers.

WOO HOO! CONVENTION DAY! LET'S GO!

TRY THIS! Conventions are a good place to sell merchandise of your comic. Try designing and ordering T-shirts of your work! Stickers and hand-crafted buttons are easy things you can make to get people excited about your comics. What else can you think of to give away at conventions?

109

MAKE A MINI COMIC

Supplies: *paper, scissors, pencil, ruler, pens, eraser*

Part of the fun of a mini comic is that you can make it quickly and get many copies to your friends and fans cheaply. Mini comics are really versatile. You can choose any size paper—11 by 17 inches (28 by 43 centimeters), 8½ by 11 inches (21½ by 28 centimeters), or 8½ by 14 inches (21½ by 35½ centimeters). You can make them by yourself or with your friends. They can be funny or they can be serious. Besides being portable, mini comics are easy to make your own.

1 Fold your paper in half three times and then unfold it completely. You have just divided your paper into eight equal sections. Each section will be a page in your mini comic.

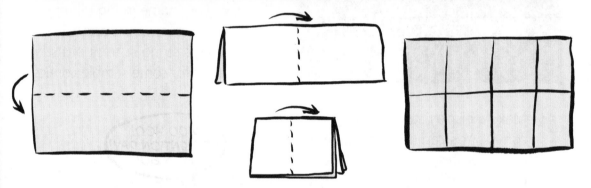

2 Fold the paper in half once along the long side and cut along the crease line from the folded edge to the center. Unfold and then refold along the short edge.

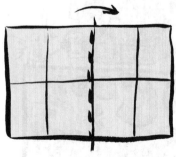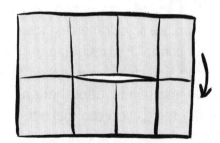

3 Pinch the sides toward the center so that the cut opens. When your hands come together, flatten all the pages to one side. You now have a mini book! Number the pages with pencil and unfold it completely.

Cover	Back Cover	9	S
1	2	3	4

4 Use a piece of scratch paper to sketch out thumbnails of your comic. What is it going to be about? What will the cover look like? Use some of the skills you have practiced in other activities to make an awesome story and cool cover.

5 Pencil your comic's art. Draw all of the art on all of the pages. If you need to, fold the pages to keep track of the order of the story.

6 Ink your comic. Erase the pencil lines when you are done. If you are going to use a color copier, you can add some color to your comic!

7 The comic art is your master copy. A master copy is the version all other copies are made from. Ask an adult to help you make your copies at a local copy store or library. When you have made your copies, follow steps one through three again to put your comics together.

8 Mini comics are like the trading cards of the comics world. If you are ever at a comic convention with independent creators, you can trade one of your comics for one of theirs. You can also share them with your friends or get a table at a convention and sell them to new fans!

TRY THIS! How can you design your comic differently? Can you use different colored paper? Try to find some friends to start a small publishing company with them. You can go to local comics conventions and sell your comics together.

MAKE A WEBCOMIC

Supplies: *pencils, paper, ink, digital camera or scanner, computer, Internet, photo-editing software such as Adobe Photoshop or Gimp*

Most comics artists use the Internet to show off their work to the global community. Others don't just show off their work, they DO their work online. These are the webcomics creators and you can be one of them. Get permission from an adult to go online and make sure you are setting up your website properly.

1 Ask an adult to help you get a website set up. Tumblr is a great place to start. Cartoonist Patrick Yurick wrote a very informative feature on setting up your Tumblr site to make a webcomic at makingcomics.com. Go to the distribution section of the website and click on "digital." Click on the "tutorial" link to access his advice.

2 Draw your comics and upload them to your website. You can either upload your comics by taking a photo of your comic or by scanning your comics into your computer. Make sure you save your image at a web resolution, which is 72 dpi (dots per inch).

3 Figure out a publishing schedule. Which days do you want new comics to show up on your website?

4 Time to promote! Tell your friends about your new webcomic and ask them to tell their friends. The online comics community likes to help each other out. Always get permission from a parent before you join any online group.

DAD, I JUST FOUND OUT THAT I HAVE FANS OF MY WEBCOMIC IN AUSTRALIA! ISN'T THAT COOL?

adaptation: telling a story in a different way and in a new format. For example, making a musical out of a series of comic strips would be adapting the comics into the musical.

afterlife: the ancient Egyptian belief in life after death.

Allied forces: the armies of the countries that fought together against Germany in World War I and World War II.

alter ego: a second personality in the same person.

American Revolution: the war during which the 13 American colonies fought England for independence. It lasted from 1775 to 1783.

ancestor: someone from your family who lived before you.

animation: multiple drawings in sequence to show movement.

anime: Japanese animation.

archaeologist: a scientist who studies ancient people through the objects they left behind.

arch-nemesis: a character who is the opposite of the main character, and usually the enemy.

aristocrat: a person of royal blood or privilege.

artifact: an object made by people in the past, including tools, pottery, and jewelry.

astrologer: a person who studies how the movements of the sun, moon, and planets affect humans.

astronomer: a person who studies objects in the sky, such as stars and planets.

backstory: a story about the events leading up to the main story.

BCE: put after a date, BCE stands for Before Common Era and counts down to zero. CE stands for Common Era and counts up from zero. These non-religious terms correspond to BC and AD. This book was published in 2014 CE.

Boston Massacre: a riot in Boston that took place on March 5, 1770. Five colonists were shot and killed by British soldiers.

brainstorm: to come up with a bunch of ideas quickly and without judgment.

broadcast: a program transmitted over a long distance.

carbon copy: an exact copy of a document made using carbon paper between two or more pieces of paper.

cartoon: a comic published in a newspaper or magazine.

cast: a group of characters.

casting: a metal print form created to make multiple copies of a printed page.

cathedral: a large important church.

censor: to examine books, movies, letters, etc., in order to remove things that are considered to be offensive or harmful to society.

character: someone in a story.

cherub: a type of angel, usually shown as a small child.

chromolithography: a color printing process using metal plates to layer tints of color.

city-state: a city and its surrounding area, which rules itself like a country.

civilization: a community of people that is advanced in art, science, and government.

cliffhanger: an exciting moment that makes you wonder what happens next.

codex: another name for a book. Plural is codices.

collaboration: working with others.

color reproduction: to make color prints of an original piece of art.

comic: images in sequence that tell a story, with or without words.

comic relief: the inclusion of a funny character or scene in an otherwise serious work.

Comics Code: a set of guidelines created by comics publishers to help regulate the content of comics.

commercial: operating as a business to earn money.

community: a group of people who live in the same area.

concentration camp: a prison where people were sent during the Holocaust to be killed or made to do hard work.

conceptualized: imagined and thought out.

content: the written material and illustrations in a story, article, book, or website.

convention: a gathering of people who are all interested in a certain idea, topic, or event.

creative rights: the right to use something that is created, often for profit.

culture: the beliefs and way of life of a group of people.

custom: a way of living and doing things, such as food and dress.

decay: to rot.

depict: to create a representation of something experienced or seen.

desktop publishing: computer software that edits and formats comics, books, and magazines.

diabolic: extremely evil.

dialogue: a conversation between two people.

digital: characterized by electronic and computerized technology.

direct mail: a system used to sell things directly to subscribers through the U.S. mail.

drafted: required to join the military.

drama: an exciting event or series of events.

dynamic: full of movement.

eccentric: odd, usually in a unique way.

emcee: a master of ceremonies who helps to lead a story or event.

epic: a long poem, usually about the life of a hero or heroine.

era: a set segment of time.

etching: a print made by scratching original art onto a metal plate.

fantasy: a genre of comics and literature based on myth and legend.

folk tale: a story told by a specific group of people, often involving magic and a moral.

freelance: to work on a project without being employed by the company assigning the work.

French Revolution: a period of violent change in France between 1789 and 1799.

funnies: the original name of comic strips in Sunday newspapers.

generation: all the people born around the same time.

genre: a type of creative work, such as mystery, romance, or fantasy.

Golden Age: the period of comics history before the 1950s, considered to be the best and most popular by many fans and historians.

graphic novel: a comic as long as a book, that tells one story.

hearing: a special session of Congress or the Senate held to "hear" from witnesses and experts on a given issue.

hieroglyphics: a writing system that uses pictures and symbols called hieroglyphs (or just glyphs) to represent words and ideas.

Holocaust: a time before and during World War II when the German Nazis tried to kill the entire Jewish race, as well as several other groups.

hometown: the place where a person, thing, or idea is born.

humor: the quality of being funny.

iconic: a widely recognized symbol of a certain time.

identity: the characteristics that make a person an individual.

image: a picture of something, either real or imagined.

immigrant: a person who leaves his or her own country to live in another country.

imprint: a part of a publishing company that publishes a certain type of book.

inbetweener: an animator who assists the head animator by drawing movements in between key frames.

independent comic: a comic book published without the help of a large company.

indigenous: native.

inking: to use ink to add definition to pencil drawings.

innovation: a new creation or a unique solution to a problem.

invincible: someone who cannot be defeated.

key frame: a drawing in animation that captures the major points of movement. For example, if a character is waving her arm from left to right, the key frames would show the arm on the left, middle, and right.

layering: stacking images on top of each other.

literate: having the ability to read.

logic: the principle, based on math, that things should work together in an orderly way.

manga: a term for Japanese-style comics.

martyrdom: the death of a person for his or her beliefs.

Marvel Method: a way of creating comics that relies on an assembly-line format.

master page: the version of a printed page that is used to make other copies.

medieval: describes the Middle Ages, the period of European history after the fall of the Roman Empire, from about 350 to 1450 CE.

medium: the material artists use to create their art, such as stone, paint, and ink.

mini comic: a small, self-published comic.

monument: a building, structure, or statue that is special because it honors an event or person, or because it is beautiful.

moral: a valuable lesson to help people know how to behave.

movable type: a process of printing that uses individual type pieces to spell out words.

mummify: to preserve a dead body so it doesn't decay.

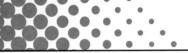

mythology: a set of stories or beliefs about a particular religion or culture.

narration block: a block of text that contains the voice of the writer or of a character talking about what is happening.

Nazi: the main political party of Germany before and during World War II.

network: a company that provides programs to be broadcast over radio or television stations.

observation: something you notice.

orally: spoken out loud.

pamphlet: an informative book or brochure.

panel: a square or other shape that frames a single scene in a comic strip.

parody: an imitation of something for comical effect.

patent: a document from the government that gives an inventor the exclusive right to make, use, or sell his or her invention.

Pearl Harbor: a U.S. naval base in Hawaii that was attacked by Japan in 1941.

penciling: to create an original comic first in pencil.

pharaoh: the title for ancient Egyptian kings or rulers.

pictographic: a picture of a word or idea.

pitch: to present an idea.

political cartoon: a comical or critical depiction of a political figure or event.

predecessor: someone or something that came before others.

premise: the main idea of a story.

preserve: to keep something from rotting.

printing press: a machine that presses inked type onto paper.

process: an activity that takes several steps to complete.

propaganda: ideas or statements that are sometimes exaggerated or even false. They are spread to help a cause, political leader, or government.

psychologist: a person who studies the mind and behavior.

Pulitzer Prize: a group of prizes awarded annually for work done in journalism, fiction, and non-fiction, as well as for photojournalism.

pull list: a list of comics that your local comic bookstore will order and set aside for you.

pulp magazine: a cheap fiction magazine published between 1896 and the 1950s.

punch line: the sentence, statement, or phrase that makes the point, as in a joke.

race: a group of people with the same skin color and other physical features.

rarebit: a type of soft cheese which is famous for giving indigestion.

Renaissance: a period of time in Europe after the Middle Ages, from the 1300s to the 1600s.

representation: showing things in pictures or other forms of art.

revolutionary: someone committed to fighting a ruler or political system.

ritual: something done as part of a religion.

romance comic: a comic about characters who are trying to find love.

Rosetta Stone: a stone tablet written in 196 BCE telling the same decree using hieroglyphics, Egyptian Demotic script, and ancient Greek. The stone was fully translated in 1822, leading specialists to understand hieroglyphics better in the nineteenth century.

saint: a Catholic Christian who has performed miracles as confirmed by the pope.

sarcophagus: a large, stone box containing an Egyptian king's coffin and mummy.

science fiction: stories that deal with the influence of real or imagined science.

screen print: to make a color print of an image with special ink pressed through screens.

scribe: a person who copies writings by hand.

sequence: the order in which something happens.

serial: occurring in a series.

serialize: to create a series of stories.

sidekick: a character who supports the main character.

Silver Age: the era of comics between the introduction of the Comics Code in 1956 and the late 1970s.

smock: a cloth worn over clothing to protect it from stains.

spiritual: religious, relating to the soul or spirit.

splash page: large pages of comic action with no panels.

standardized: a set way of doing something.

stylize: to draw comics in a specific way.

suspense: a feeling or state of nervousness or excitement caused by wondering what will happen.

symbol: a physical representation of a thing or idea.

syndication: when the rights to print or broadcast a creative work are sold.

tapestry: a colorful, woven fabric that hangs on a wall. It often shows a scene.

technology: scientific or mechanical tools, methods, and systems used to solve a problem or do work.

thought cloud: a shape similar to a word balloon that encloses a character's thought.

tint: a shade or variety of color.

tomb: a room or place where a dead person is buried.

tribe: a large group of people with common ancestors and customs.

vigilante: a person who takes the law into his or her own hands.

villain: a character who opposes the hero and does bad things.

Wacom tablet: a device that allows an artist to draw life-like lines right onto a computer.

webcomic: a comic made to be read on web browsers.

woodcut: a way of printing by carving an image on a piece of wood before adding ink and printing the image onto paper.

word balloon: a rounded outline with a point toward a character that encloses the character's speech.

xerography: a way of making a copy using light-sensitive chemicals and paper.

zine: a self-published magazine, usually produced using photocopiers.

zinester: a person who makes zines.

Books

Cartooning the Head and Figure. Jack Hamm. Grosset and Dunlap, 1967

Comics and Sequential Art. Will Eisner. Norton Press, 2008

Comics, Manga, and Graphic Novels. Robert Petersen. Praeger Books, 2011

Dick Tracy: American's Most Famous Detective. Bill Crouch Jr. ed. Citadel Press, 1987

Expressive Anatomy for Comics and Narrative. Will Eisner. Norton Press, 2008

Graphic Storytelling and Visual Narrative. Will Eisner. Norton Press, 2008

How to Draw Comics the Marvel Way. Stan Lee and John Buscema. Simon and Schuster, 1984

How to Make Webcomics. Brad Guigar, et al. Image Books, 2011

Men of Tomorrow. Gerard Jones. Basic Books, 2004

Reading Comics. Douglas Wolk. Da Capo Press, 2007

The Comic Book History of Comics. Fred Van Lente and Ryan Dunlavey. IDW, 2012

The Comics: An Illustrated History of Comic Strip Art 1895–2010. Jerry Robinson. Dark Horse Comics, 2001

The Ten-Cent Plague. David Hajdu. Picador Press, 2008

Understanding Comics. Scott McCloud. Kitchen Sink Press, 1993

Primary Source QR Codes

Page 24: upload.wikimedia.org/wikipedia/commons/4/40/1896-11-08_Yellow_Kid.jpg

Page 27: en.wikipedia.org/wiki/Mutt_and_Jeff#mediaviewer/File:Muttandjeffalla51.jpg

Page 28: ignatzmouse.net/us/archives/kk

Page 30: comicstriplibrary.org/display/111

Page 32: youtube.com/watch?v=xH9tCcrrcak

Page 48: images.tcj.com/2014/01/SuperDiscov2.jpg

Page 50: youtube.com/watch?v=GJCTTba4S0E

Page 56: youtube.com/watch?v=vr9qpeOjmuQ

Page 70: loc.gov/exhibits/blondie/wedding.html; blondie.com

Page 71: peanuts.com

Page 72: youtube.com/watch?v=dS0vUbWdNxg

Page 83: youtube.com/watch?v=1jgE-lrfZ3k

Page 93: garfield.com; zenpencils.com/comic/128-bill-watterson-a-cartoonists-advice

Page 94: calvinhobbesdaily.tumblr.com

Page 104: lastpolarbears.com; garfield.com; littledee.net

Page 108: rhymeswithorange.com; baldocomics.com/blog; getfuzzyarchive.blogspot.com